DUBLIN
OLD AND NEW

STEPHEN GWYNN

Dublin: BROWNE AND NOLAN LIMITED
London: GEO. G. HARRAP & CO. LTD.

7LM
14.7.38
mullan
be/s.

Made and Printed in Ireland by Browne and Nolan Ltd.
The Richview Press, Clonskeagh

AUTHOR'S FOREWORD OF ACKNOWLEDGMENT

THIS BOOK owes much to the splendid publications of the Georgian Society, and to Dr. Chart's admirable *Dublin* in the "Medieval Cities Series." I acknowledge a more personal debt to Mr. C. P. Curran, who, in revising the proofs, gave me the full benefit of a knowledge much more thorough than my own.

Dr. Best and his assistants at the National Library have been most helpful, as is their excellent custom.

With regard to illustrations, I have to thank the Board of Governors and Guardians of the National Gallery of Ireland and the Curator of the Municipal Gallery for their courtesy and goodwill in permitting reproduction of several of their pictures. The Provost of Trinity College has allowed me to reproduce the portrait of Dr. Salmon and to photograph the State Drawing-room, and the President of University College has permitted reproduction of his own portrait by Sir W. Orpen and Mr. Whelan's portrait of Father Finlay. I have to thank Mr. Charles H. O'Conor, President of the Irish Association of the Knights of Malta, for photographs of Lucan House and demesne illustrating one of the finest examples of Georgian architecture, and the Secretary and members of the Old Dublin Society for allowing me to have photographs taken during their exhibition at Charlemont House of the Smock Alley passes, Sarah Curran's locket, and the No Rent Proclamation.

I also thank Mr. Francis ffrench Davis for permission to photograph the Salmon Pool; Dr. Leeper for permission to photograph his Swift souvenirs; Mrs. James MacNeill for the photographs taken during her husband's tenure of office at the Viceregal Lodge; Mr. John McCann for the illustration of Portobello Lock; the " Irish Press " Ltd. for photograph of the Kettle Memorial; the Harry Clarke Studios for photograph of a stained glass Window, and the Librarian of Trinity College for leave to photograph a page from the "Book of Armagh." The *Irish Times* has supplied a photograph of the Army Jumping Team; Miss Purser, a photograph of a stained glass Window manufactured by An Túr Gloine. Mrs. W. R. Nolan has let me have the landscape painting of the Sugar Loaf by Mrs. Lennox Robinson; the Corporation of Dublin and the Librarian, Kevin Street Public Library, have lent the print of Zozimus.

FOREWORD

I owe special thanks to the lady whose portrait shares a page with the portrait of Curran, and to Mrs. Mitchell for her two admirable Dublin types.

Most of the photography is the work of Mr. Hubert Heasler, whose skill and patience has greatly enriched the book, but Mr. B. Aitken's camera study of St. Audoen's Gate deserves separate acknowledgment.

My last word of thanks is to the friend whose help in collecting illustrations has brought me privileges which I could never have secured for myself.

CONTENTS

LIST OF ILLUSTRATIONS

LIST OF ILLUSTRATIONS

CHAPTER I

DUBLIN OLD AND NEW

THIS book is meant to serve, more or less, as a guide to Dublin; but it is just as well to be outspoken. Those who come for a brief visit to the city and want to know what to look at in a few days will find it best to consult the chapter headings, or go straight to the later part, which I hope will suggest, with a reasonable degree of intelligence to the reasonably intelligent, how a short time may be spent in and about Dublin.

But frankly, if it is Dublin itself that interests the visitor, you cannot see Dublin that way. All cities have more in them than meets the eye, a guide is needed in all ; yet some carry their story and their romance on the face of them—Prague and Budapest, or, a better example and nearer home, Edinburgh with its castled crag. Dublin cannot compete with these in picturesqueness ; it lies on the level, it sprawls about its river mouth, it is built mainly of greyish yellow brick, drab in effect, though under some shifts of the Irish sky it can take the colours of a pigeon's breast. Those who have the taste for eighteenth-century architecture will recognise it at its best in Dublin ; but say what one will for it, eighteenth-century building does not stimulate the imagination.

Besides, even when the most splendid of these buildings were taking shape, Dublin as a whole had, by the repeated asseveration of its own Press, a bad name for dirt. " Dirty Dublin." That is far less true to-day than in times I can remember ; but at best to-day its aspect makes a drab impression.

It is true that this picture with its low tones is approached among the most winning prospects, and is set in every variety of natural beauty. Mountain and plain, wide stretches of vivid grass-land, high slopes purple with heather or golden with gorse, are to the westward, and east is blue sea and yellow strand ; and over all the moist Irish air with its pearly illumination on a day of sunlight can transfigure even the grey city and give magic to the river between its long quays.

But the true brilliance of Dublin, its only brilliance, comes from people who have lived there ; and they are not all dead. Comedy and Tragedy have chosen it many times for the theatre where farcical happenings and high romance were always ready to jostle each other. O'Casey's plays are a living witness to what we all remember, not twenty years ago ; and if he avoids romance, though surely not sparing of tragic colour, yet what in the world's history was ever more romantic than the gesture of a few young men who challenged England when she had a million of men in arms, and died, and won by dying ?

For those who think that the talk in O'Casey's plays is too highly-coloured, I would quote a couple of chance observations. One comes from a Dublin cook, when a well just outside the city had run dry and she was heard complaining : " There's not as much water in the house as would baptise a fairy, and me with the potatoes to put down for dinner." Another was from a workingman, who described his ganger as " that lazy he wouldn't lift a hand to turn a red herring on the griddle ; but he'd ask me to shift the rock of Giberalther."

Of course these flowers of speech are not so plenty as dropped papers in the gutter ; one should not expect too much. An Englishman crossing from Holyhead with a Dublin Judge said how delightful it must be to live in a town where everyone was so witty. " Ah, nonsense," said the Judge, who was an Ulsterman with an Ulsterman's robust idea of pleasantry, " if you come to dinner with me, I'll find you a dozen people as stupid as yourself."

All parts of Ireland bring their own quality into this melting pot : Dublin is the compendium of Ireland. What it is to-day has taken a long time in the making ; and to appreciate what it is and what it keeps, one must at least know something of the past.

Old Dublin has memories and associations going back for a thousand years ; it is an ancient city. But as a capital it has a peculiar character. London existed centuries before English was a spoken speech ; the French language and France itself were formed about the living germ that was Paris. Dublin was founded as a stronghold of heathen invaders, many generations after Ireland was known throughout Christendom for a centre of religion and learning—when Ireland had already its fully developed language, its literature cultivated by a professional class of poets, its system of law expounded by elaborately trained lawyers. The law that was administered from Dublin was never Irish law. When Dublin became officially a capital, it was the capital of a Norman-English kingdom, that claimed authority over the whole island but often could scarcely make its writ run over three or four counties. Even after the conquest was completed, and Dublin began to be a metropolis, the government which had its seat there was from century to century governing Ireland without the consent of the Irish people.

But according as Dublin became more and more the vital centre of Ireland, it became more and more the heart of resistance to England ; and it was in Dublin that the rebellion broke out which at last made Dublin the seat of a native Irish government. That revolution has given us a new Dublin, whose history is not yet twenty years old.

It is not yet the seat of government for all Ireland. More than a quarter of the Irish people are, by the will of a local majority in the North-

East, under a separate Irish legislature. That partition may last long : we in Dublin are sure that it will not last for ever. The upholders of a separate State for six Ulster counties think themselves just as Irish as the Irish Protestants of Grattan's day did who voted for independence. Outside of Ireland, beyond all Irish jurisdiction, millions of men and women scattered over the world claim Irish blood, whether it be to their advantage or disadvantage ; and for the Irish at large, in Ulster or in the Free State, in Ireland and out of Ireland, Dublin is beyond yea or nay the capital of Ireland.

It is really far more Irish than Connemara or any other part of the Gaelic-speaking seaboard, because it represents more fully the mixed race which the Irish are to-day. In 1937 when a new Irish Constitution was being prepared, Mr. de Valera, as head of the government, proposed that the Gaelic word *Eire* should be adopted as the official name of the country. It was the Lord Mayor of Dublin who immediately objected : " Ireland," he said, " is much a better known name." Certainly, to the world at large Dublin will still be the capital of Ireland.

Why it became the capital, why it became the capital of an invading power, is easily explained. The Irish were formidable pirates in Roman days, and St. Patrick, son of a Roman citizen in Britain, was captured in one of their raids. He escaped and returned to convert his captors ; Ireland took enthusiastically to Christianity and to Christian learning. Whether that was the cause or no, they certainly became less piratical : and piracy is the primitive form of sea power. Ireland had no strongholds on the coast. The sea was a barrier to them when it was an open road to the vikings from Denmark and Norway. These raiders and traders, working along by Orkney and Shetland and the Isle of Man, came down St. George's Channel, and established posts at estuaries and inlets : Waterford, Wexford, Arklow, Wicklow, Carlingford, Strangford, are all Danish names. Dublin was the central point on the coast, and over and above the Liffey mouth there were good landing-places on Howth and at Dalkey. Howth is also a Scandinavian word " Hovud," a head-land. To this day the people of that countryside say *Hoadh*. The Irish name for the headland is Benn Edair. Dalkey is half Irish—Thorn Island— *Dealg Innis* in Gaelic. But " eye," as in Ireland's Eye, is the word whose diminutive is eyot.

Probably there was already a village about where Dublin stands, because the main road into Wicklow from Tara crossed the Liffey by a ford at the head of the tideway, where a hurdle bridge was constructed. The place was called *Ath Cliath*, the Hurdle Ford, and the Gaelic name for Dublin was, and is, *Baile Atha Cliath*, the Town of the Hurdle.

6

Dublin is a Gaelic name too, *Dubh Linn*, the Dark Pool, and the Danes soon knew that name. History of cities is generally determined by river courses, and the Liffey made Dublin. If you look from the Phoenix Park, you will see how it comes in from the plains west of the city, through a well-defined valley, with high ground on both sides. Seawards, the ground on the north bank slopes down till it is little higher than the river ; but on the south a high ridge continues, roughly parallel to the stream but drawing closer to it, until Christ Church stands at the top of a really steep ascent. The river swings in naturally under this bank ; but where the ground opened level on its left bank, water got room to spread and there was a shallow where the hurdle ford crossed. Bridgefoot Street, running down sharply from the ridge, indicates the place.

But a little further down, where Grattan Bridge faces the end of Parliament Street, there is a reef of rocky formation in the muddy river-bed ; and below this again you may see at low water the overflow of a small stream, now covered over for much of its course, the Poddle. It ran on the inner side of the high ridge, and its junction with the Liffey was just below where the rock reef cramped the water coming off the shallow. Thus there was formed the kind of long deep tidal pool familiar to every angler about the mouth of most salmon rivers.

The Danes rowed their galleys up here, and the point of the ridge with the water on both sides was easily stockaded. That was the beginning of Dublin.

Gradually the wooden enclosure extended as the town grew in importance ; a bridge was built across the river for convenience. But the town was still confined to the south bank. It did not remain wholly Danish : the invaders married Irish women. Gradually too, after a hundred years of oppression, the native race struck back in the open field. Finally Brian Boru, King of Thomond, asserted his supremacy against Malachy of Meath and was accepted as High King of Ireland. But he took also Malachy's wife, Gormlaith, formerly wife of the Dane who ruled in Dublin. Later, he cast off this fierce queen who, by her marriages, had allies of Danish blood and Irish blood ; and the end was a great trial of strength when " the foreigners of Ireland " summoned the foreigners from overseas to help in a fight for the mastery of Ireland. It was a great viking muster, and the issue was tried out at the gates of Dublin on the sandy shore by Clontarf, on Good Friday in 1014. But there were Danes in Brian's army, from Limerick and Waterford, and there were Irish also on the side of the foreigners. Long ago, an old friend of mine, an ex-Fenian, said to me : " I will tell you what I would not tell to many. The ——" (and he named his Leinster clan, whom I shall not name) " were on the wrong side at Clontarf."

KILLINEY BAY

THE MOST FAMOUS DUBLIN CITIZEN
LORD MAYOR BYRNE

Brian was victorious, but before the day was over, his son and his son's son had fallen, and in the confused fighting Danish fugitives came on the old King praying for victory. One viking turned on him, and Brian slew, but was slain. After that day, the Danes never attempted conquest of Ireland ; but they remained in their towns—probably not unwelcome, for they had most of the foreign trade and the Danes of Munster paid Brian a yearly tribute of a hundred tuns of wine. In Dublin at all events they had become Christian, and the Danish ruler of Dublin founded what is now Dublin's oldest monument, Christ Church Cathedral.

Outside the walls, beyond the Poddle stream, a level space of ground stretched towards the bay, covered with grassy hummocks, the Hogges. It came to be called Hoggen Green. The biggest of these, at the top of what is now Suffolk Street, was used as the Thing Mote or Danish open-air parliament.

Irishmen and Danes were more and more intermingled, and in the middle of the twelfth century Dermot MacMurrough, King of Leinster, presented a tract of ground about what is now College Green to the Augustinian monks, on which they built their monastery of All Hallows. From that foundation Trinity College was later to arise and Hoggen Green was to be College Green.

From Dermot MacMurrough came the invitation

which brought in the first Norman invaders. They conquered a good deal of Irish territory and they conquered what was even more important, the still Danish towns of Wexford, Waterford and Dublin. Then came Henry II in person and definitely fixed on Dublin as his capital. There is no question but that the Irish rulers at large agreed to be included in his empire, which then stretched from York to Bordeaux. But the Norman invasion of Ireland was very different from that of the Danes. Like the Danes, they had the sea power ; but they wanted the land as well. They built in stone for defence ; they built the Castle ; they walled in Dublin ; they dammed the Poddle to make a moat on the south, and Dame Street, which leads from the Castle to College Green, is really Dam Street. A mill was driven by the overflow, somewhere about the present gate into the Lower Castle Yard.

But the Normans were great church builders. They rebuilt Christ Church on the Danish foundations ; some people hold that the crypt is the Danish church. Strongbow is buried in the tomb there, under a recumbent armoured effigy. Not content with Christ Church, they built a second cathedral outside the city walls, beside an old well sacred to St. Patrick. It seems to have been held that the native population, part Irish and part Danish, had too much hold on Christ Church.

CHAPTER II

DUBLIN in the Norman days was not really Irish. Citizens were imported from Bristol and given a charter with the same rights as Bristol enjoyed. Still, they developed a thing which was new in Ireland—settled urban life. One condition of that life is a water supply, and Dublin, with the hills so near it, is singularly well placed for this. A charming little river, the Dodder, comes down out of the beautiful Glenasmole (or Thrushes Glen) and falls into the Liffey at the tideway. So far back as 1220 the citizens put a dam across the Dodder above Templeogue, and led a water-course from here into the bed of the Poddle, doubling or trebling the flow of that little stream.

But if the neighbouring hills were convenient in this way, they were a menace also ; for this range of wild mountain, forty miles long, remained outside British law for many centuries ; and its people, the O'Byrnes and O'Tooles, nearly wiped out the colony from Bristol, a generation after it was founded, by a raid one Easter Monday while these citizens had gone out to disport themselves at a bowling match in Cullenswood—now called Ranelagh, part of the suburb of Rathmines.

Medieval Dublin was kept close within the ring of its walls : the western gate stood on the ridge near where Guinness's Brewery now covers many acres, the eastern just by the Lower Castle Yard.

In Tudor days, under Henry VIII and Mary and Elizabeth, the capital was less menaced and rich men began to build houses on the level towards Hoggen Green. The monastery of All Hallows had been confiscated, and under Elizabeth it was decided at last to provide Ireland with a university. Trinity College was established on the site of MacMurrough's foundation. So came into being an institution most intimately linked with the life of Dublin.

It was planned on the pattern of Oxford and Cambridge—and designed to be one college with resident students in a university of several colleges. But College and University have remained a unit. From the first Trinity was a home of scholarship, and even of Irish scholarship ; Archbishop Ussher made a great collection of Irish manuscripts and left it to the University. But the same learned Ussher was one of a Commission appointed to put down all teaching that was not Protestant, and he himself has recorded how in Galway they found a school with a thousand scholars who answered very well in Latin, and how, because Lynch the teacher was a Catholic, they disbanded the school.

From the beginning of the seventeenth century,

when English rule was at last thoroughly established, Dublin began to be a real capital, and also
the seat of a university. But the Catholic gentry
of Ireland had to look outside of Ireland for
education and for employment. The separateness
of Dublin people, according to where they
go to church, had its deplorable beginning
then.

In the seventeenth century the prevailing idea
was to root out the Irish and plant the country
with English. Vast confiscations of land led
inevitably to a rebellion in 1641, which became
entangled with the English struggle between King
and Parliament. Twelve years of devastating war
followed and Kilkenny became for a time an Irish
capital; but Dublin remained in English hands. Its
population, never large, shrank at this period to
less than 9000.

After the Restoration there was a period of
peace, and the Duke of Ormonde governed Ireland
as Viceroy. He was head of the great Anglo-
Norman family which for long centuries contested
supremacy with the Geraldines of Kildare.
Under his auspices the city spread fast ; its
numbers reached 40,000 before the Revolution and
the flight of James II.

Ormonde did well by Dublin. Outside the West
Gate, at Kilmainham, there had been established
in the thirteenth century a monastery of the
Knights Hospitallers, a military order (still histori-

cally represented by the Knights of Malta, whose members may be seen at times in Ireland, wearing a most decorative costume). After the suppression of the monasteries, Kilmainham was at times used by the Viceroys as a residence : but it became ruinous till, in 1679, Ormonde, by Charles II's authority, rebuilt it as a hospital for veteran soldiers : The Royal Hospital, designed by an Irish contemporary of Wren's, is a fine example of seventeenth-century architecture.

Change is marked here. Until 1922 it was still a hospital for Irish veterans, and in a house off its pleasant quadrangle was the residence of the Commander-in-Chief of the British forces in Ireland. There is now no such office in the Free State and the Irish regiments are all disbanded, except two which have their depots in Ulster : and the place is occupied as the headquarters of the new Civic Guard. But the Hall is still there and well worth seeing—rich in carvings, attributed to Gibbons, but work of a Dublin sculptor.

Yet Dublin owes more than that to Ormonde. He enclosed the Phoenix Park—at first it is true as a hawking ground for the Viceroys, their residence was then at Chapelizod, in the Liffey valley. But this great enclosure soon became what it has remained, a superb pleasure ground for the people of Dublin.

Until Ormonde's day, the city was practically confined to the south bank. Under him new

14

bridges was built and streets planned, along where Ormond Quay keeps his name.

South of the city, pastures extended to the little river Dodder, which falls into the Liffey's estuary. About sixty acres nearest the city were a common for the citizens, and the Corporation marked off half of this for building lots, in a square, keeping the centre open, and enclosing it with a ditch and a line of trees. It was stipulated that the houses should be at least two stories high, of brick or stone. But Stephen's Green was never uniform in the character of its buildings, like the squares planned in the eighteenth century. It remained patchy even after much rebuilding ; and its first inhabitants seem to have been of the citizen class. Grafton Street was a lane leading to it from Hoggen Green, and in 1671 " so foul that people could not walk in it."

But the movement for richer people was in the other direction ; the north side became inhabited. Four new bridges were built. Essex Bridge, now Grattan Bridge, was the most important ; streets led direct to it from the Lower Gate of the Castle. The line of it northward was continued by Capel Street, and streets were built east and west parallel to the river—still on the low ground. About 1725 much more ambitious building was undertaken further up the slope ; Henrietta Street became the centre of fashionable residence. In another twenty-five or thirty years, the upper part of the slope was covered with fine streets which extended towards the sea—streets that are now in lamentable decay. Residential Dublin has moved decisively to the south and south-west.

That movement began only about 1750 when the Duke of Leinster built his new house in Kildare Street. Merrion Square grew up beyond it. These two fashionable quarters, about Henrietta Street and Stephen's Green, were as far apart as Belgravia and Bloomsbury : in addition, they were divided by the river. But Dublin had then a formed, polished and elegant society, with its own distinctive quality. I cannot find any trace of that before the eighteenth century ; though the man who helped most perhaps to shape it was born in the reign of Charles II, a few years after the wars of Cromwell's time.

One extraordinary feature of the period was that so many men had become soldiers as to leave Ireland short of lawyers. Four brothers of an English family named Swift, two of them barristers, two solicitors, came over to seek their fortune—and on the whole were not disappointed. One of them, Jonathan, died young, leaving a posthumous son to inherit his name ; but an elder brother, Godwin Swift, could afford to bring up the boy, who was sent first to Kilkenny school and then to Trinity College, where he was not happy—or lucky. Jonathan Swift was perhaps never happy or lucky ; but few names are more famous, and in reality the

Z O Z I M U S
(MICHAEL MORAN).

ZOZIMUS—All my buzzum friends are turned backbiters. The nearest and dearest must part. And he scattered the seeds of the unrighteous over the face of the earth, and he crushed them with his all mighty power. Is there any tinder-hearted Christians round me? Yez all remimber what Saint Paul said in his Epistle to the Romans (for he never wrote to the Protestants), a ha'penny will neither make you nor break you. Is there any blackguard heretics listenin' to me now?

Come all ye heretics, by faith forsaken,
That sell yer sowls for a pound of bacon,
Come listen unto me, one and all,
And I'll sing you a song called Farnham Hall.

Now, my barrikin quildrivers, have yez no other devarshin only sticking pins in a dark man; if the watch was set, or the "new polis" out, I'd make sum av yez jump Jim Crow.

PHOTOGRAPHED FROM AN ORIGINAL SKETCH BY GRAY.

PUBLISHED BY JOSEPH TULLY, 58 MIDDLE ABBEY-STREET, DUBLIN.

REGISTERED.

THE MOST FAMOUS OF DUBLIN BALLAD SINGERS
Died 1834.

FLYBOAT IN THE LOCK AT PORTOBELLO

From an old print.

history of the Dublin that we know begins with him.

It was he who taught the Anglo-Irish, and more especially the Anglo-Irish of Dublin, to think themselves a nation, and a nation that should be free. It was he also, one of the world's best letter-writers, who left us in his correspondence and stray writings a vivid picture of those times. Of famous Dubliners he should be counted the first. After two centuries he is still a legend. "Very classical, ma'am, as classical as Dean Swift." That was the highest term of praise employed by the lady in my household who complained that she had not enough water to baptise a fairy.

The Dublin of O'Casey's plays is the same Dublin that Swift lived in ; and though Dublin is a city of many fine buildings, many stores of treasure, with magnificent " outsports " (if I may use an Irishman's word) all about it, the real fascination of Dublin is in the life and the tongue and the brains and the friendliness of its people.

From Swift's time onwards, that Dublin began to be itself as we know it. There has been change, of course, and growth and decay—growth in some directions, decay in others—during these two hundred and fifty years. But throughout them all the Capital of Ireland has set its own stamp on men who came from all corners of Ireland, and indeed from other countries, to various destinies. Edward Carson from County Galway was a

3   17

Dubliner as much as Timothy Healy from County Cork. And how hard it is to shake off the trace of your origin may be observed in every page of the writings of Mr. George Bernard Shaw. He has lived most of his long life in London, but London and the world owe their debt to a Dubliner.

CHAPTER III

CENTRAL DUBLIN

I HAVE sketched an outline ; let me fill in some detail.

A thousand years ago, as we have seen, Dublin was a huddle of buildings in wood, or wattle and daub, stockaded at the seaward end of the ridge which runs along the south bank of the Liffey.

Three hundred years ago—when Strafford ruled for Charles the First—the city was still all on the left bank, but had spread westwards along the ridge, and eastwards on to the flat land about the present Dame Street and College Green.

Two hundred and fifty years ago—when Ormonde ruled for Charles the Second—rapid growth had begun ; five bridges connected the two banks and Dublin was growing fast on the north side.

One hundred and fifty years ago Dublin ranked among the more important capitals of Europe. It had about two hundred thousand people and was roughly a third of the size of London. A splendid residential quarter had grown up on the north side, at some distance back from the river ; another, about the same distance, had developed on the south bank. But the main feature of the present city was not completed till the great boulevard of Sackville Street was carried down to the river and joined by a fine bridge to another wide straight thoroughfare, Westmoreland Street.

As Dr. Chart has put it, the backbone of Dublin lay originally east and west, parallel to the river. Now it lies north and south, across the river. The two lines intersect in College Green, which is the centre of modern Dublin.

A circle of half a mile radius drawn about this centre includes the Parliament House, the Castle, the Mansion House and the City, the chief banks and the chief shopping centres, the main hotels ; it includes the cathedrals, the universities, the picture galleries and the museums—it takes in also the port. Roughly, all that is of interest for a visitor to see in the city lies in this small compass.

But the residential quarters and the suburbs lie outside it. That on the north side, which was splendid a hundred years ago, has lapsed into squalor. Dubliners who could choose their place of residence have moved more and more south along the line of the shore, and south-west towards the foothills of the mountains.

If you stand at the gates of Trinity College, Grattan's statue faces you, opposite the old Parliament House, which is now the Bank of Ireland. Beyond the statue a wide straight street runs west and at the end of it you can distinguish rising ground—the end of the ridge on which Dublin began. On top of this rise is Christ Church ; to the left of it is the Castle, and beyond the Castle, on the low ground inside the ridge, is St. Patrick's.

A long street, which has several names in succession, but was in reality the old High Street of Dublin, runs westward from the open space between Christ Church and the Castle ; its irregular waving line is the mark of its age ; short steep laneways, rather than streets, run down from it to the south quays. It passes what is still called St. James's Gate (though no trace of the gate remains) where the air is heavy with the reek of malt from Guinness's great brewery. Beyond this, on the right of the main road leading to Kildare, are the Royal Hospital, and Kilmainham Jail ; nearer to the river is Kingsbridge Station. But the railway terminus belongs of course to the nine-teenth century, and so does the King's Bridge, named in honour of George IV.

Nothing along this line to-day beyond the Castle counts in the social life of Dublin : and although Dame Street still holds some of the best shops, the streets between it and the river have no very metropolitan appearance. But in 1780, when eighteenth-century Dublin was fullest of vigour, this district, from the Castle to the Parliament House and along the quays, was the very centre of city life.

To-day Dublin Castle is little more than a group of departmental offices : the state-rooms are only on rare occasions used for entertainment. Even before our revolution the social functions of the Viceroyalty were mostly held in the Viceregal Lodge, away in the Phoenix Park. But in 1780 the Court lived in the Castle, and Dublin's theatres were as near the Castle as the Haymarket is to St. James's Palace. The Theatre Royal was in Crow Street, which leads from Dame Street to the river : but the part where the theatre stood was so close to the river that it has now been cut off. The rival house was in Smock Alley, a street that exists no longer ; it led out of Fishamble Street, which comes on a slant from Christ Church Place to what is now called Grattan Bridge. In Fishamble Street there was an assembly room where Handel chose to have his "Messiah" performed for the first time.

Look at this quarter now and judge of the change. Garrick acted here, they all acted here, and probably the greatest actress of that century—certainly the one I should most like to see brought back to life—began here ; Peg Woffington was a Dubliner born.

Yet in this very corner of the oldest Dublin one of the most characteristic expressions of Dublin's life can be seen, on certain occasions, at what is now the Olympia Theatre : earlier generations knew it as "Dan Lowry's." Its repute was then not of the discreetest, and to-day it does not hold the most fashionable of Dublin audiences. Workingmen and workingwomen with their families crowd at cinema prices to see their idol " Jimmy O'Dea," when he puts on a panto-mime at Christmas. Another Dublin man, Mr. O'Donovan, writes the words, though I daresay the comedian makes his own of them. Desire to see Mr. O'Dea in song and dance and to hear Dublin backchat about all the topics of the day in Ireland has spread so far that he has at times taken the Gaiety, Dublin's most " regular " theatre (a theatre of illustrious memories) and filled it. But his fame was won in the shabby little house that lies between lanes that were crowded when Smock Alley competed against Crow Street.

One of these lanes beside the Olympia Theatre leads into Crampton Court, a real piece of old Dublin. In this tiny square used to be the Little Dublin Coffee-House and the Exchange Coffee-House, much frequented by business men in the time (about 1765) when the Royal Exchange was built up against the Castle wall. The Exchange has served for generations as the City Hall, where the Dublin Corporation transacts its business, and affords much occasion for Mr. O'Dea's peculiar gift.

All anglers used to know Crampton Court because Mrs. Garnett's fishing-tackle shop was there. That centre of attraction has been moved from the old Court to Parliament Street, a broad thoroughfare from the foot of Cork Hill opposite the Lower Castle Gate to Essex Bridge—now called

Grattan Bridge. But you may still go through Crampton Court to a side-entrance of the Dolphin Hotel, whose smoking-room an intelligent foreigner once described to me as the only surviving example of an eighteenth-century tavern or coffee-house— when taverns and coffee-houses were the clubs of the times.

It is more easily approached from Parliament Street, which leads from Dame Street opposite the Lower Castle Yard to Grattan Bridge. When that bridge was built, the line beyond it was continued by Capel Street, then considered a very smart thoroughfare. But on the south bank, approach to the river led through old and narrow ways ; so Parliament proposed to open this wide passage. Some householders refused to budge, even for good compensation ; men were sent by night to pull the slates off their roofs and they had to go. The name of the street shows Dublin's approval of the proceeding.

Beyond yea or nay, a hundred and fifty years ago the Parliament House was the centre of Dublin society ; it had even more the quality of a club than the London House of Commons. Sir Jonah Barrington tells us that in every session, when the finance estimates were submitted, there were two days of purely formal proceedings, carried out by officials. On those two days the Speaker invited the whole Assembly to dinner, without distinction of parties or persons ; and they drank and joked together without a word of controversy. On the third day, the House went into Committee, and Opposition speakers, Grattan, Curran and the rest, set about tearing the estimates to pieces and denouncing the government as worthy of impeachment.

Duels often sprang from a debate, but after any more than usually acrimonious interchange the Speaker always took steps to see (if possible) that antagonists were bound over to the peace ; to avoid this it was necessary to slip out quietly, and this was not always accomplished. One famous duellist (a judge), observing himself pursued by the officials, bolted ; his coat-tails were caught by the door as he slammed it and he tore himself free—only to be arrested and brought back into the House. The hilarity which his appearance occasioned there did much to appease the quarrel.

But the Houses of Parliament had a sort of annexe where no such interference had to be dreaded. Just outside the precincts on the same side of College Green the building which is now the Yorkshire Insurance Office was then Daly's Coffee-House, which served as a fashionable club. Gaming ran very high there, even for a gambling age. From it a concealed passage led to the House, and members who wished to avoid the tedium of debate spent their time (more profitably or not, according to circumstances) over cards, from which they could be summoned if a division grew imminent. In a paragraph in the *Evening Post* of November 21d, 1782, a writer describes how (when debates on the question of Irish Independence ran high) he was "sauntering near the door of a certain coffee-room" and observed "a few straggling majority members taking a repast. They scouted by turns from stuffing to know whether the question was going to be put. On being told that a certain patriot was about to speak, 'Oh,' said one, 'that's a fine long-winded fellow ; we may take another bottle or two.' "

There was great stir of life in the streets between Dame Street and the river and along the quays in those days. The city was ill-lit, ill-paved and ill-policed. One constant cause of turmoil was the "black cart," sent out by the Corporation to arrest beggars : it moved with an armed guard, there were many flights from its approach, and many rescues. On the quays hackney coaches stood, drawn up by the river wall ; but the drivers preferred to sit on the pavement opposite, with their legs stretched out as an obstacle to passers-by ; and they were more importunate even than the beggars. Any well-dressed person was beset with suggestions that he should treat himself to a ride : if he declined, the jarveys ran along after him, and entreaties soon turned into taunts on his meanness.

Another obstacle to peaceful circulation of which correspondents to the Press complained were the ballad singers. Every occurrence of the day was

strung into verse and sung by these strollers. It
might be the story of an abduction, it might be
the proposal of some unpopular measure in
Parliament. Swift let loose whole flights of them
against " Wood's halfpence," light missiles to
support the formidable onslaught of his prose
invective. Goldsmith, when he was a student
at Trinity, wrote ballads, partly to get the five
shillings which he badly needed, but chiefly to
enjoy the delight of standing by to hear his own
words sung. At any time of political excitement
Dublin newsboys take up a good deal of the
pavement, but these were newsboys who sang the
print that they sold. Capel Street, Essex Bridge,
each end of Parliament Street, and all the length
of Dame Street were " infested " with them from
dark till ten at night " so that it is difficult to
pass along the flagged way, such crowds assemble
about them, by which many gentlemen lose their
pocket-books, watches and handkerchiefs."

Hangings, which provided so popular a diversion
in London of that day and were specially patron-
ised by men of the highest fashion, like George
Selwyn, do not seem to have been so popular in
Dublin. The gallows hill was beyond Stephen's
Green, near where Leeson Street approaches the
canal. Possibly prudence kept the well-to-do away,
since it is complained that " rioters practised
slinging paving stones at the hangman, pursuing
this useful though contemptible member of society

with implacable resentment "—and not caring much whether the paving stones hit the hangman or the public. It was a tough age. There is a description in 1776 of an execution (not in Dublin, it should be said, but from the wilds of County Galway) where the hangman enlivened the proceedings by appearing dressed " in the highest female *ton*." " The curls, lappets, ribbons and all the flowing equipment which renders the appearance of our fashionable ladies so formidable were gibbeted by the grim journeyman of death."

From that period when, as one poet of the Press wrote,

> Curls monstrous, curls insulting, stand
> Like mountains piled by giant hand,

it may be of interest to quote an advertisement dated 1777 :—

To the Ladies.

The Tête Warehouse (being the only one in this Kingdom) is now completely furnished with every assortment of Ladies' Headdresses in the present fashion by ENGLISH, Ladies' Hairdresser, No. 28 Nassau Street.

Notwithstanding the envious Reports of the many *flying Têtemakers* and Hairdressers who would insinuate that the said ENGLISH buys bad Hair, he can assure the Public that such Report is false and done to prejudice him in his business on account of his Moderate Prices for ready Money.

28

	£	s.	d.
The new Buckingham Curls, Long Neck and Side Curls		1	7
Sistems, so light as not to be felt on the Head		2	8
Ditto, covered with long Hair . .		4	10
Back Bows, very full of Hair . .		2	8
Plain Shanoes 1/1, and if covered with long Hair		2	8
Plain Têtes from 3/3 to . . .		5	3
Ditto and two Curls . . .		7	0
Ditto and four Curls . . .		8	8
Full dress Tête		11	4
Natural Edge Tête with two Curls each side and not to be distinguished from the natural Head of Hair, from 5/5 to .		14	1
Long Bredes from 5/5 to . . .		16	3
Ladies' Wigs, not to be distinguished from the natural Head of Hair, from 11/4 to .	1	2	9

N.B.—As the fashions change, he will alter all the work bought from him.

All country commands punctually obeyed by receiving a pattern of the Hair. Gentlemen's wigs at the usual moderate prices ; and his Dressing Rooms continued at the Rere Door of the Four Courts for the Convenience of Gentlemen of the Law.

One feature of old Dublin has been revived in the new. In Grattan's day every paper was full of advertisements of lotteries, often promoted by government as a means of raising the wind. To-day the Hospital Sweep, launched by authority of the Dublin Parliament, has the proportions of a government department. And the processions through the streets before each big drawing of the lots are modern Dublin's only substitute for such pageantries as amused the public when the Corporation used to " ride the boundaries."

Social life in Dublin has moved away from the neighbourhood of the Liffey, where once it centred. The Castle has an unpopular name and is never likely to get over it. A native Irish government, receiving guests there on ceremonial occasions, as it must do, has always about it some suggestion of masquerade. Up till the most recent phase of revolution, Nationalist Ireland always talked sentimentally of " re-opening the old House in College Green," and putting a new Irish legislature where Grattan's parliament sat. But when the final revolution came, sentiment had changed, too, and there was need for something immediately available. By accident, perhaps, rather than design, the seat of the legislature has been moved in accordance with the general drift southward. The Bank of Ireland remains in possession, it is faced across the street by other great banks, and Grattan, in Foley's bronze, maintains his declamatory gesture between temples of the money changers.

Trinity College remains, as before, with its gates opening on the very centre of the city's traffic, an element inextricably associated in the city's being. The Four Courts, some considerable distance away on the north side of the quays, pin down a considerable part of Dublin's energies and interests to the banks of the Liffey. But nearer to the actual centre, on both banks of the river, are the great newspaper offices which in all capitals create about themselves a district of Bohemia. Nobody who has read any of the novels which depict the life of modern Dublin will underrate the importance of its pubs : and it is safe to say that the most celebrated of these institutions are to be found not far from the quays.

Clubs have moved. The frequenters of Daly's Coffee-House transferred themselves to Kildare Street a century before Parliament itself went there. Four others—the University, the Stephen's Green Club, the United Services, and the Friendly Brothers of St. Patrick—have their habitation in fine old eighteenth-century mansions along the side of Stephen's Green, where the Shelbourne Hotel stands. The United Arts Club is still further away south, in what is still purely a residential quarter, about Fitzwilliam Square ; and it would certainly claim to have close alliance with whatever in Dublin is Bohemia.

But every true Dubliner will agree that pubs have counted for more than clubs in the social life of many who left the deepest mark on the life of Dublin—from Clarence Mangan, whose bust stands in Stephen's Green, down to Tom Kettle, whose bust now makes a pendant to face Mangan's. Kettle, wit, orator, essayist and poet, was the delight of all companies—in the House of Commons, or the mess of the Dublin Fusiliers, with whom he met his death on the Somme, but most of all in the little Dublin hotels or bar-rooms which journalists and their congeners frequent. They might lie as far towards Stephen's Green as one of the side issues off Grafton Street ; they might be on the line of O'Connell Street, or of Dame Street. I associate Kettle most with the Dolphin's smoking-room ; but he might as readily have been met in the Moira, in Trinity Street, a favourite haunt of James Winder Good, the best journalist I ever knew in Ireland and the friendliest human being. Or at "The Bailey" in Duke Street, where Arthur Griffith was a constant diner—the most powerful political writer that Dublin has known since the days of Swift, and the one whose writing produced most consequences. Griffith has the best right to be regarded as the father of Sinn Féin.

Dublin's pubs were and, I suppose, are, the equivalent of Parisian cafés. Literary groups, artistic groups, political groups, had their regular or irregular meeting places in them. And in so far as they reflect the most active intellectual life of Dublin, it cannot be said that its centre has shifted far from the quarter where life was most crowded in Grattan's day. But I have to deal now with the quarter from which all flush of what was once splendour has faded and left decay.

MEMORIAL BUST OF T. M. KETTLE
By Albert Power, R.H.A.

DUBLIN BAR—TWENTIETH CENTURY

DUBLIN BAR—EIGHTEENTH CENTURY
JOHN PHILPOT CURRAN

By Sir Thomas Lawrence R.A.   National Gallery, Dublin.

CHAPTER IV

THE NORTH SIDE

UNDOUBTEDLY the focal point of Dublin is College Green, where the main lines of traffic east and west along the Liffey, north and south across the Liffey, meet and cross.

It is a meeting place of memories as well. In 1782 an Irish Volunteer force in uniform paraded here to celebrate the gaining of Ireland's independence, under Charlemont and Grattan. That independence was lost in 1800. In 1923 Irish Volunteers, who had regained independence, marched in a new uniform past the President of the Irish Free State as he took the salute from the steps of Ireland's old Parliament House.

As a political centre College Green has lost its significance and has a new emotional appeal. The Bank of Ireland on one side and the National Bank and Ulster Bank facing it mark the tender spot where we keep our overdrafts.

One historical landmark has disappeared. The first statue erected in Dublin was the equestrian group showing King William III on horseback in front of the Parliament House. Patriots of Grattan's day paraded yearly on King William's birthday. When they placarded one side of the

pedestal with " Free Trade or This," pointing
to the cannon below, the other side had for inscription " The glorious Revolution." In short, they
were good Williamites. In the course of the nineteenth century King William came to be less
regarded in Dublin as a natural centre for patriotic
demonstrations, and more than once the statue
was contumeliously bedaubed. But while British
rule lasted it stood. Very soon after the Free
State's beginning, some patriots of the newer type
contrived to put a bomb under it ; and this
ancient landmark was taken away—leaving to
Grattan undisputed possession of the field.

Grattan's statue has links with nationalist history
much later than Grattan's own day. After 1867
Fenian prisoners of importance were being moved
from one jail to another in Manchester ; a rescue
was undertaken and succeeded, but in bursting
the prison van the rescuers shot a police sergeant
dead, and three men were convicted of having
taken part in the attack. Each of them, as sentence
of death was passed on him, made the same
answer, " God save Ireland ! " and " God save
Ireland," written by T. D. Sullivan, became the
rallying song of Irish nationalists till " The Soldier's
Song " took its place.

A. M. Sullivan, another of the same famous
family, was then editor of *The Nation*, and agitated
for a public funeral procession in Dublin, which
was held, as the Government thought, seditiously.

Sullivan was prosecuted and sent to jail for incitement to sedition. So was another journalist, Richard Pigott. Readers of *The Nation* raised a fund of £400 to indemnify Sullivan ; he refused to accept it, but proposed to make it the nucleus for a statue to Grattan. The commission was given to Foley and the monument in College Green is the very fine result. But at that procession in 1868 John Martin, who had been one of the " Young Ireland " rebels in 1848, was present, and he met there a young Wicklow squire named Charles Stewart Parnell, who was beginning to appear on Nationalist platforms. Martin liked him and took steps so that, when he died in 1875 Parnell succeeded him as member for County Meath.

Richard Pigott also reappears in the Irish story. He forged the letters by which it was sought to implicate Parnell in the Phoenix Park murders ; his confession and suicide marked the height of Parnell's triumph. So the links of memory are knit over Dublin's central space.

But perhaps the point from which to begin looking at Dublin is O'Connell Bridge, especially in the afternoon, when a westering sun makes the Liffey shine with reflected colour. The long line of the quays is pleasant and the Four Courts show up handsomely ; on the south bank Christ Church can be seen on top of the ridge. The curious in such matters will find many attractions in antique shops on each side, and the open air bookstalls used to be nearly as frequent as those along the Seine. Edward Dowden, for many years professor of English Literature in Trinity, when he was writing the *Life of Shelley*, picked up in a two-penny box what was then the only known copy of a pamphlet. Later he found another ; bargains, but deserved, for no one else would have recognised these as Shelley's *Proposals to form an Association for the Regeneration of Ireland*, addressed to the people of Dublin, encouraging them to revolution. Shelley was then twenty and lodged, with his wife Harriet (aged seventeen), in the second house from the river on the east side. The actual house is gone, for most of that broad street was destroyed either in 1916 or in 1922. Shelley knew it as Sackville Street and the bridge as Carlisle Bridge ; and so did everybody else till after 1880, when the O'Connell monument, facing the bridge, was set up. The first marking date in the long Irish revolution is 1829, when O'Connell carried " Catholic Emancipation," and got leave for Catholics to sit, not only in Parliament, but on the Dublin Corporation. That body in Grattan's day was much less Irish in spirit than the Parliament, and much more completely opposed to Catholic claims. Their attitude is sufficiently expressed by the fact that Nelson's Pillar was planned to dominate Dublin's finest street. But in 1880 Parnell had arrived, and the new wave of revolution had begun which broke the landlord power. It is a mark of the time that the Dublin Corporation not only decided to place the Liberator's memorial there, but to rename after him both street and bridge. There are still people who say " Sackville Street " on principle, and some who prefer it for euphony. The same used to be true about Carlisle Bridge, but I found the other day that a lady, after twenty-five years of life in Dublin, had never heard it called anything but O'Connell Bridge.

When the O'Connell monument was unveiled amid great crowds, a Dublin jarvey was heard to cry out : " Now, Nelson, you have your match." And certainly it is not Nelson who has won.

Artistically the O'Connell monument, though a fine group, is not comparable in interest to the three great portrait statues by the same artist which adorn College Green. The Parnell monument at the other end, by a famous American sculptor, St. Gaudens (son of an Irish mother), has never been counted a happy example of his work. Artistically, indeed, the street offers nothing excellent, and much of the rebuilding has been ill-conceived ; only the noble spacious proportions of the original plan are to be praised. But O'Connell Street, with its range of statues and its recent associations, gives a summary of a hundred years in Irish history.

Two strands throughout that history are closely

intertwined. O'Connell, for the first time, organised the mass of the Irish people politically. His astonishing eloquence roused them to join in a vast association and to use their votes at the open ballot, defying the threat of eviction. Monster meetings were held all over the country ; it is said that one at Tara brought together half a million men. Finally, when O'Connell, a Catholic, was returned as member for County Clare against a powerful landlord, it was clear that England must either give Catholics full citizenship or face insurrection ; and the Duke of Wellington yielded.

O'Connell went on to demand Repeal of the Union and restoration of the Irish Parliament. He had the nation with him. One rich Irish landlord, Smith O'Brien, of the family that had ruled in North Munster since the day of Brian Boru (and long before it) was member for County Limerick and joined him. A group of able young men, led by Thomas Davis, John Blake Dillon and Charles Gavan Duffy, founded a paper called *The Nation*, which ran like wildfire. The verse in it, collected as *The Spirit of the Nation*, was even more influential than the prose.

But soon a divergence set in. O'Connell preached an absolute refusal to use physical force. He was a constitutionalist by nature, and hated bloodshed, all the more because a duel had been forced on him—as a means to get rid of the Catholic champion ; he shot his opponent D'Esterre dead, but for ever after wore a black glove on his right hand.

The men of *The Nation* group—" Young Ireland " as they came to be called—set their faces against this doctrine. They held that a nation had a sacred duty to assert its freedom in arms. Ireland in 1840 had eight million people, half the population of Great Britain ; and they were organised though not armed, and stronger because more sober. Father Mathew, the Franciscan, had then launched his temperance crusade.

Then came in 1846 potato disease, bringing famine ; in 1847 it was at its worst and people died by tens of thousands. Smith O'Brien, who had taken his part with Young Ireland, broke completely with the British Parliament, of which he was a member, and came over to join the desperate men. In 1848 a tide of revolution swept over Europe and Ireland was caught by it ; but the rising was half-hearted ; the priests, who had taken O'Connell's side, opposed it. Smith O'Brien headed insurrection mainly on a high point of honour and the defeat was ignominious.

In the years that followed, the constitutional movement was taken up again, seeking to act through Parliament. From 1860 onwards, Isaac Butt, a brilliant lawyer, who had at first opposed O'Connell, became the leader in demanding what was called " Home Rule." Yet the physical force men, bitter over their failure in 1848, never accepted defeat, and a new secret organisation, the Irish Republican Brotherhood, spread, chiefly in the artisan class. They were generally known as the Fenians, and after the close of the American Civil War they found experienced soldiers ready to lead them. The Fenian rising in 1867 was no more successful than that of 1848, but it alarmed England. Mr. Gladstone introduced the Bill which ended the established privileges of the Irish Protestant Church.

The Fenian Society was driven underground : many of its members suffered long imprisonment. One of these was Tom Clarke, who on coming at last out of jail, set up as a tobacconist and news-agent a few doors out of O'Connell Street, round the corner from the Gresham Hotel. That shop was a centre of propaganda during a full gener-ation. It was the nursing home of the 1916 revolution.

But another phase of the struggle had inter-vened. Michael Davitt was the son of an Irish cottier, who had been evicted from his holding and had gone to England for work. The son grew up in Lancashire. Fenian organisation had spread among the Irish in England, and young Davitt, though he had lost an arm in some accident with machinery, took part in an attempt to seize Chester Castle. He came out of jail after ten years, deter-mined to apply in Ireland the methods of trade unionism—and also to cement friendship between the English and the Irish democracy. No Irishman was ever more free from rancour.

By that time a young Protestant landlord, Charles Stewart Parnell, had entered Parliament as a member of Butt's party and began to challenge Butt's too easy-going leadership. When Davitt advocated a Land League, which should be virtually a trade union of tenants for resistance to rackrents and eviction, Parnell threw himself in with it : and Davitt's influence brought over to Parnell most of the Fenian element, suspicious though they were of parliamentarians. The movement for Home Rule was now united to a movement which would give the Irish tenant a lasting right to his holding. Davitt stood in with it, heart and soul. He wanted to destroy " feudalism " in Ireland.

Fierce agitation was accompanied by boycotting (the word came in then), and by outrage and murder—just as in the English trade unionist struggle of early days. The political leaders were put in jail as " suspects," and from Kilmainham Jail Parnell issued a " No Rent " manifesto. By 1885 the landlord power was broken, and at a general election Parnell carried eighty-five in a hundred of the Irish seats ; Gladstone introduced his first Home Rule Bill, which was beaten in the Commons. But the struggle went on hopefully till the famous " Parnell split."

In that schism, most of the country turned against Parnell, but Dublin stood solidly by him. In 1892 Gladstone's second Home Rule Bill passed the Commons, but was defeated in the Lords. The constitutional struggle went on and in 1911 the absolute veto of the Lords was taken away. A new Home Rule Bill had a great majority for it. Then began the raising of volunteers in Ulster, pledged to resist Home Rule by force. In October, 1913, a counter force of Irish Volunteers was launched at a meeting held in Dublin. But the English Government, afraid of civil war—since the whole Conservative Party were backing Ulster— proposed to leave six Ulster counties out of the Bill. Redmond, for the sake of peace, agreed to this as a temporary expedient, but Irish opinion was violently against it. Then, in August, 1914, when the Home Rule Bill was about to be presented to the Lords for the third time—after which they could not prevent its passage—the European war came suddenly, and all the English parties agreed to drop their differences.

Redmond was in a desperate dilemma. He might unite England in antipathy to Ireland. He might let civil war of the most savage kind loose in his own country. On the other hand, he hoped that if Irish troops from Ulster and the rest of Ireland fought side by side, old hatreds might disappear, and the cause for partition vanish. He pledged the support of Ireland to England in defence of the general cause of freedom. All natural sympathies of Ireland were on the side of France and Belgium, and Nationalist Irishmen in tens of thousands answered Redmond's call to arms. His brother and his son were in an Irish Division which was formed, as counterpart to the Ulster Division.

But the Fenian organisation, which had always maintained a secret existence, held to the old principle that England's difficulty was Ireland's opportunity : and a large section of the Irish Volunteers determined to act " for Ireland only " —and against England. The English Government, which had allowed the Ulstermen to arm and drill openly, did not feel justified in suppressing this other force. Meanwhile Roger Casement, a man famous for courage and ability, was trying to bring about a German landing to serve as a spearhead for revolt.

A rising was planned for Easter, 1916. But Casement, who had decided that insurrection without serious foreign support would be hopeless, was on his way in a German submarine, nominally to help the rising, in reality to call it off. He was seized in Kerry on Good Friday and taken to London. The news spread and the heads of the Volunteers countermanded the muster.

Yet a group of men in Dublin, including the old Fenian, Tom Clarke, but headed by a poet-schoolmaster, Padraic Pearse, and half a dozen others (two of them also poets), decided that unless blood was shed for Ireland in Ireland, Irish nationality was doomed. Disobeying orders, they called out the Dublin battalions of the Volunteers, and on Easter Monday suddenly occupied buildings all over the city. Pearse made the General Post Office his headquarters and from the steps of it he proclaimed the Republic. Four days' fighting followed, in the course of which most of O'Connell Street was destroyed.

Nothing could have seemed madder. England had more men under arms than at any time in history. In Ireland the troops were practically all Irish and they attacked the rebels without hesitation. Men fought on opposite sides who had been comrades in the Irish Volunteers. Dublin had sent a whole brigade of Dublin Fusiliers to the Irish Division, and the people were for the troops : when the fight was over, the prisoners were insulted in the streets. A month later, as they were being transferred to England, they found themselves cheered.

Pearse, an idealist and mystic, had never hoped to win. But he reckoned that England would so deal with the situation as to put Ireland on his side. That is what happened. An officer in the Irish Division came back from France a fortnight after these events and a very shrewd Irishman said to him : " The fools : it was the first time in history that a rebellion had the people of Ireland against it and they turned them round in a week."

All this A B C of modern Irish history must be acquired by anybody who wishes to understand what is to be seen in Dublin's greatest street. Smith O'Brien now has his statue there, behind O'Connell. He was sentenced to be hanged, drawn and quartered, the usual sentence for high treason, but was reprieved and transported with several of the younger leaders to Australia. It is amusing to remember that at the time of his trial, his elder brother, Sir Lucius O'Brien of Dromoland, was seeking to establish in the House of Lords his claim to the barony of Inchiquin, granted to his ancestor by Henry VIII. Naturally enough he thought that the rebel had not improved the chances of his suit. But the House of Lords did not allow political feeling to interfere with genealogy.

Sir John Gray, who is next in the rank, was a Home Ruler of an early period—editor of the *Freeman's Journal*, a paper that (with fluctuations) supported the national cause from 1750 till about 1925, when it disappeared—too closely associated with the name of Redmond's party to be popular.

In 1912 the whole length of O'Connell Street was so packed with a demonstration in support of Redmond and the Home Rule Bill that you could have walked on men's shoulders from end to end of it. In 1917 Redmond was being hooted in the streets.

The Gresham Hotel was for many years a sort of headquarters for the Nationalist Party : Redmond always stayed there. The offices of the United Irish League were just opposite.

Father Mathew has his statue—a lamentably bad one—also near the Gresham, in what the eighteenth-century Dublin called The Mall. He belongs more properly to Cork than to Dublin ; yet his mission was to all Ireland A charming social personage, of good family (with near relations deriving their wealth from a brewery) ; yet he decided to become a Capuchin friar in the Franciscan Order, and for quarter of a century he was ministering unobserved in Cork—no preacher, but a magician in the confessional. " The worse you were in the beginning, the better he'd like you." The poor worshipped him ; and in private he was a delightful host, loving to entertain his friends, not without whiskey punch.

But at public committees for the prevention of misery, the drink question was never out of sight ; and there was always a short stout Quaker who would rise and say, " Ah, Theobald Mathew, if thee wouldst take the matter up ! " Finally the priest sent for the Quaker and said he was convinced : there was a meeting held in Father Mathew's schoolroom, and with a blank roll of paper before him, saying " Here goes," he signed his name first, taking the pledge to abstain from all alcohol. That was in April, 1838, and by

December there were 150,000 names on the roll. Then it was announced that he would administer the pledge in Limerick, and people realised at first what was happening when the crowds nearly trampled each other to death. When he travelled by mail coach from Dublin, the mail car was kept five hours late. Bianconi, who ran the car, answered protests by giving Father Mathew a free pass for all journeys at his pleasure.

The whiskey that had paid duty dropped in five years from twelve million gallons to five ; but Roe, the great Dublin distiller, sent Father Mathew a large cheque towards a church he was building, saying that no one had done him so much harm, but it was nothing to the good he had done to Ireland.

The apostle went north, where sectarian feeling was savage, and one man, after taking the pledge and getting the blessing that went with it, stood up and said, " Ah, Father, you'd not be blessing me if you knew I was an Orangeman." " God bless you, my dear, I would not care if you were a lemon man."

The Famine broke Father Mathew as it broke O'Connell. One of his early efforts had been to get Cork a new graveyard. In June, 1848, the new cemetery had to be closed : ten thousand were buried there in nine months. His fight now was not with drink, but with famine ; and paralysis struck him. He died in 1856, and his face in death was like that of one in torture.

He deserves a better statue than he has either in Cork or in Dublin ; but it would be worse if Ireland had no memories of him.

Pearse has no public monument in Dublin ; but the General Post Office serves for one. Scores of books have been written about the four days' fighting which centred round that resistance. But from College Green to Westland Row is now Pearse Street, because the workshop was there in which Pearse's father carried on business as a stone-cutter and mortuary sculptor. He was English, married to an Irishwoman. The son became known first as editor of the Gaelic League's Journal —a courteous, quiet and likeable young man. He left his post to start a school where all the teaching should be given in Irish—first at Cullens-wood House, near Ranelagh Station where, in the eighteenth century, Dublin had its imitation of the London pleasure grounds. Then he moved out to the Hermitage, beyond Rathfarnham—changing the name to St. Enda's : attracted there by the association, for this was near the Priory, where Sarah Curran lived, whose love letters were found on Robert Emmet when he was taken.

The poems of Pearse, and of his two comrades, Thomas MacDonagh and George Plunkett, who signed with him the proclamation of the Republic, would have interest even without the tragic

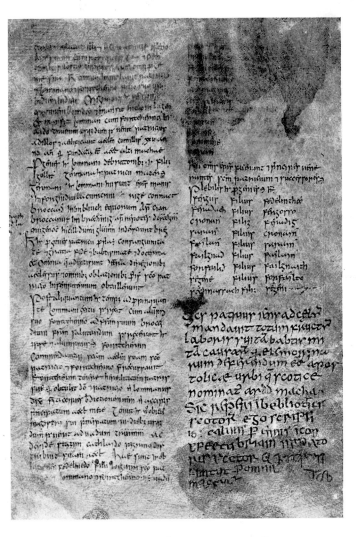

PAGE FROM THE "BOOK OF ARMAGH"

The larger writing is the entry made on a blank space in the Book in presence of Brian,
confirming the prerogatives of the See of Armagh. The last distinct lines read " Ego
scripsi i.e. Calvus Perennis in conspectu Briain imperatoris Scotorum "—I Calvus
Perennis wrote this under the eye of Brian, High King of the Irish.

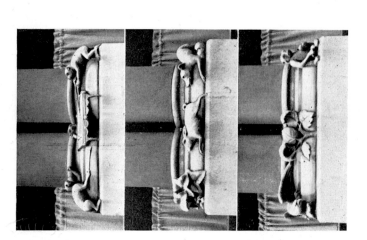

STONE CARVING BY THE O'SHEA BROTHERS ON THE KILDARE STREET CLUB AND ON THE ENGINEERING SCHOOL, TRINITY COLLEGE.

consecration given to them by a firing party.
In O'Casey's play, *The Plough and the Stars*,
one passage from a speech that Pearse delivered
is introduced—as heard, though the speaker is not
seen. The later stages of the revolution and the
early stages of self-government called out qualities
in other men which Pearse might not have possessed.
But I think no man in Ireland but he could have
launched the revolution as he did, or on so high
a pitch ; and the memory of 1916 is not disfigured
by ugly deeds.

The revolutionary party which came to be
called Sinn Féin sprang out of the Gaelic League,
founded to be unpolitical. Both the language
movement, and the movement away from parliamentary politics began in the time after the Parnell
split, when Ireland was sick of politics—or wanted
politics of a new kind. Another movement that
issued from that same period has its lasting monument just off O'Connell Street, in the Abbey
Theatre. Yeats, at the suggestion of Lady Gregory,
set the thing moving. After a couple of failures
with English actors, they found the nucleus of an
Irish company in the brothers W. G. and Frank
Fay. The theatre was given to them by a generous
Englishwoman, Miss Horniman ; but before they
had it, Irish plays played by Irish actors had been
recognised in London as well as in Dublin for a
new thing in the dramatic world.

To Yeats above all Dublin owes its Irish theatre ;

but the sombre genius of J. M. Synge gave actors and actresses a greater scope than any dramatic work by Yeats. Nothing in the early years was so well known as Synge's *Playboy of the Western World*— partly because Dublin audiences at first resented it as a libel on Ireland. Dublin owes it to Yeats that he insisted on producing Synge's work again and again till it won favour. But Lady Gregory, who shared the direction with Yeats and Synge for many years was, perhaps, most indispensable of the three. She turned her hand to everything, wrote tragedy or comedy as it was needed, and always with a happy distinction. No visitor to the Municipal Gallery should miss Epstein's portrait bust of this gifted woman. An excellent painting of Yeats, by one of the younger artists, Seán O'Sullivan, R.H.A., hangs over the box office in the Abbey.

Actors and actresses came and went, the theatre could not pay large salaries ; but the supply of talent has seemed inexhaustible, after nearly forty years. Yet, until after the war, the Abbey's patrons came mainly from the most fastidious public in Dublin. After the war Dublin saw revolution, years of curfew and street fighting ; and then a Dublin workingman produced plays in which the humours and tragedies of Dublin in the throes of revolution were rendered with genius. All Dublin, rich and poor, crowded to see Seán O'Casey's *Shadow of a Gunman* ; the Abbey began to turn money away. Then came *Juno and the Paycock* with Miss Sara Allgood in the chief part, and actors with her only less amazing than she was.

O'Casey's visions of Dublin in that period have the peculiar stamp of revolutionary madness on them : broad farce set against the awful sight of a mother crying over her dead son. But if those who see O'Casey's plays compare them with the pictures of Dublin in Joyce's books, in Gogarty's *As I was Walking Down Sackville Street*, in Liam O'Flaherty's *The Informer*, or in Conal O'Riordan's *Adam of Dublin*, they will find the stamp of the same city on them all.

The Abbey Theatre is, take it all in all, the most notable thing that modern Dublin has to show. For one cannot separate Yeats's lyrical poetry from his dramatic work ; and scores of Irish authors have contributed to the theatre's long list of productions. St. John Ervine and Lennox Robinson not only produced plays there, but have had much to do with the management. To-day the Board of Directors include the poet F. R. Higgins, and the novelist Frank O'Connor.

Moreover, the Abbey Theatre serves as central office for a new body—the Irish Academy of Letters, launched by three outstanding men, Shaw, Yeats and " Æ," but including from the first all the young creative artists. The building (it used to be the city Morgue) has no attraction, but visitors to it will see in the entrance hall portraits of the people concerned with its early successes—most of them painted by John Butler Yeats, the poet's father.

This is not the only theatrical attraction on Dublin's north side. Part of the old Rotunda Buildings is now the Gate Theatre, where two actors of talent, Hilton Edwards and Michael MacLiammóir, started another repertory theatre whose aim was to produce modern plays, not exclusively of Irish authorship. A change was intended from the Abbey's comedies of Irish life in villages and slums, and its tragedies based on the Gaelic mythology. Lord Longford, who supported this enterprise, proved himself a notable playwright, over and above his other help. Many plays by modern authors, English and Continental, were given, and not a few of Shakespeare's—with the result that the Abbey Theatre also was induced to vary its routine in the same way. Perhaps the younger intelligentsia of Dublin finds the Gate more interesting than the Abbey and certainly is grateful to the company for having been much more inventive in the lighting, scenery and general production. But in fact Dublin has now two local schools of admired acting, and when either company goes on tour abroad, as often happens, substitutes of surprising excellence are produced in these very fine theatres. Perhaps, as a consequence, the best English companies are seldom seen at the old Gaiety Theatre, where Irving and

Ellen Terry, Sarah Bernhardt, and their rivals, often drew great houses.

But I must get my review back to the eighteenth century.

John Beresford, the Chief Commissioner of Customs, in 1755 had a fine house in Marlborough Street, near Tyrone House, which belonged to the head of his family; meanwhile he planned—against much outcry—the building of a Custom House on superb lines, and provided in it separate apartments for the Chief Commissioner. Generations of Beresfords were born there. The chief building contractor was an Englishman named Lever, who married an Irishwoman; their son, Charles Lever, entered Trinity, qualified there as a doctor, but before he was thirty grew famous for rattling novels of Irish life. Until a time that I remember, Lever was regarded as the Irish novelist *par excellence*.

There is much to be said against John Beresford. He did as much as any one man to undo Grattan's work and to sow permanent hostility between Catholic Ireland and the English. As a long deferred result of his political work, the class to which he belonged has lost every jot and tittle of its power in Ireland, and not a little of its prosperity. But he had a sense of splendour, and Dublin owes him perhaps the finest of all its eighteenth-century buildings.

The Custom House was burnt in 1920 when the

Irish Republican forces were striving to make English rule impossible : the object was to destroy the paper records necessary for tax collection. Happily the architect Gandon's plans had been preserved, and the building, remodelled inside, has lost none of its outward beauty.

The Four Courts also felt the flames. After the Treaty of 1921 had been accepted, a section of the Republican forces refused to recognise anything but the Republic. They seized the Four Courts, held it and mined it. When at last the Free State Government, headed by Griffith and Collins, took action, an attack on the Four Courts was the opening ; and before the garrison was driven out, an explosion destroyed the records of centuries. Here again rebuilding has been possible on the old lines, but irreplaceable documents vanished in cinders.

As before, the Four Courts are set like a four-leafed shamrock about the central hall under its great dome : only that now a fifth and more august leaf is added for the Supreme Court.

Originally, the main traffic of the place was transacted in the Hall ; solicitors, barristers and their clients moved in a whirlpool round a central statue of Justice. Justice, however, in the course of time was transferred (I do not enquire for what reason) to the front of the King's Inns, where she presides over the final stages of Irish legal education —the earlier ones being given in the universities.

A suitable meeting place and home of study for the barristers was provided in the Law Library, for in Dublin lawyers do not have separate chambers as in England. This was upstairs in the old building ; now it is approached by a passage leading past the Supreme Court. In the wide corridor, tables are set where solicitors and barristers converse with their clients. A door at the end leads into the gowned and bewigged assembly : a doorkeeper bellows the name of the desired barrister who arrives, and if the conversation is to be on business, it is transferred to the corridor ; for inside are only the privileged—enclosed, as I have heard it said, like microbes in a septic tank, mutually assailing and destroying each other.

I was well received there by reason of my profession ; the assembly was still gnawing the bones of the latest literary libel ; and expectation of new provender was in all those gleaming eyes.

One feature of the new Dublin was notable. In the room where a friendly guide received me, we were alone for a moment ; then came a knock at the door and a young lady entered, with smart efficiency written all over her well-attired person. She asked for details of a case pending, got them and vanished. That, I was told, was a solicitor's clerk. I was told also that in old times a solicitor's clerk was a creature whom you might send about his business with small ceremony ; now, as I saw, you must open the door to let them out. Indeed no self-respecting man could do less, unless it were to pray for prolongation of the visit. In the *sanctum sanctorum* itself, the Law Library, here also were the ladies, not in neat tweeds, but in extremely becoming wig and gown. I wished that I could conjure up the shade of John Philpot Curran, or even Lord Morris of Killanin, to hear the utterance of an earlier day on these phenomena.

Associations of the Four Courts are too many to review. All the greatest Irish advocates for a century and a half have pleaded there, and the Library, which serves as a common-room, has brought Irishmen of opposing creeds and politics into close daily association. It has less of the sectarian division than any other centre of Dublin's social life—unless possibly the Labour headquarters. Timothy Healy and Edward Carson became friends there as well as opponents. Of the two, Carson, from Galway, at school and college in Dublin, was more of a Dubliner than the schoolmaster's son from Bantry Bay in West Cork, who began independent life as a ticket clerk on Tyneside.

One curious fact of the new Ireland and the new Dublin is that eloquence has disappeared. There is no Irishman in Dáil Eireann (the Parliament) or in the law courts who has the name for moving speech which, in Grattan's day, Curran perhaps had beyond all others at the Bar, and which many had in the generation to which Healy and Carson belonged.

Before leaving the city's north side, visitors might glance at Liberty Hall, the corner building which stands opposite the hideous iron bridge which blocks Dublin's view of the Custom House. History has been made here. In 1913 one of the most remarkable strikes in Irish records was fought from there under the leadership of "Jim" Larkin— who is still a force in Irish politics. In 1916 James Connolly made Liberty Hall the headquarters of a Citizen Army which supported the Irish Volunteers. Connolly, on behalf of Irish Labour, signed the proclamation of the Irish Republic along with Pearse ; along with Pearse he fought through the defence of the Post Office and along with Pearse was sentenced to the firing party. Liberty Hall remains the centre of the Irish Labour movement, which stands a little apart from the ordinary Irish nationalism that is partly *bourgeois* and partly peasant in its outlook.

CHAPTER V

DUBLIN MOVES SOUTHWARDS

OLD Dublin reached its climax in the time of what we call Grattan's Parliament—though Grattan was only the outstanding figure in a brilliant group. The period was at its height for the twenty-five years before 1800, when the Union took away the parliament which was the reason for that group's existence. In that period the most exclusive club in Dublin was the Granby Row Club. To-day many Dubliners could not tell you where Granby Row stands.

It forms the west side of a square originally called Rutland Square, after a Lord Lieutenant of the period ; new Dublin names it Parnell Square, because the Parnell monument stands near the corner of it, just where a gentle slope of ground begins, after the long level of O'Connell Street.

The beginning of this square is characteristic. Dublin's maternity hospital was in South Great George's Street which leads south-west from Dame Street. It was cramped for space in this crowded area near the Castle and Dr. Bartholomew Mosse, a public benefactor, undertook the provision of a new hospital. He acquired a space of land on this slope beyond Sackville Street and began to build the new hospital at the lower edge. But money did not come in easily, and he had the idea of financing the charity by a clever use of the land, building at the corner of his plot the Rotunda Assembly Rooms, which were to be what Vauxhall was to London. The space behind was laid out as a pleasure ground : Granby Row, a street of fine houses, was built on the west of it, running up the hill northwards ; another street opposite continued the line of Sackville Street. Facing the pleasure grounds from the crest of the slope, and looking out over the city to the mountains, Lord Charlemont, one of the richest and most cultivated nobles of that day, built Charlemont House. Other houses to right and left of it were added, in such a style of splendour that this northern side of the square was called Palace Row.

Happily decay in this quarter has been averted. The Rotunda, where balls innumerable were given in the eighteenth century, has lost its social prestige ; and the lines of its fine front are abominably defaced by advertisements. But the hospital, which has long been called after it, "The Rotunda," is not only alive, but so powerful that medical students from England come over by hundreds to complete their training there. And although Granby Row and Palace Row are no longer the choice abode of peers and members of parliament, Charlemont House has been remodelled internally to house one of the best things that Dublin can show—its Municipal Gallery of Pictures.

In the Rotunda itself political memories have overlaid the social ones. In Grattan's day, Grattan and his party claimed that Ireland's parliament should be freed completely from English interference. The claim was refused till a Convention of the Irish Volunteers met in Dungannon and demanded freedom in the name of eighty thousand men in arms : and within two months the Irish Parliament, on Grattan's motion, carried the same demand unanimously : in six weeks it was conceded by the English Government. But more was needed, and the Volunteers continued to press especially for a reform which would have made the parliament truly representative—as it was not.

Again a Convention was summoned, this time in Dublin : it sat in the Rotunda, while Parliament sat in College Green. Flood, who was now at the head of the movement, came from one assembly to the other, bringing down the heads of a Reform Bill to which the Volunteer assembly had agreed. But parliament refused to accept dictation from an armed body ; Flood's motion was rejected and the Volunteer body, led by Lord Charlemont, a man of peace, submitted. Nationalist Ireland has always held that the Volunteers should have persisted, and that Flood was right. At all events the association of that building with the Volunteer movement remained in memory, and in October, 1913, when it was proposed to raise an Irish

Volunteer force as a counterpoise to the Ulster Volunteers, the plan was launched at a meeting in the Rotunda ; and Redmond, like Grattan, held aloof. Recent Irish history, and the whole of the final revolution, may be said to date from that meeting, over which Professor Eóin MacNeill, Vice-President of the Gaelic League, presided as chairman.

So the new links up to the old. In 1782 the Rotunda was in full vogue as a fashionable assembly. But fifteen or twenty years earlier, when Mosse began to build his hospital, and when Charlemont planned his great house, this was a new area.

But to understand the development of Dublin on the north side, one must consider the bridges. The oldest of all, where the Hurdle Ford had been, was west of the Four Courts ; the second, known as Bloody Bridge, still further west.

Until after the Restoration in 1660 these were the only bridges. Under Ormonde's rule, the number was brought up to five. Bloody Bridge was still the furthest up river ; but Essex Bridge, close to where the Custom House then stood, was built in 1675. Dublin preserved the memory of what it owed to Ormonde by calling the quay here after him. Capel Street continued the line of Essex Bridge northward ; Abbey Street ran off it, parallel to the river. But fashion moved towards higher ground and in 1720 Henrietta Street, well up on the slope, was planned on a larger scale

61

and here the most important personages had their residences.

Chief of these was the Archbishop of Armagh. For the first half of the eighteenth century Lord Lieutenants made only occasional appearances in the Irish capital. Government was carried on by Lords Justices, one of whom was always the Primate. The last of these dignitaries, who to our mind seemed very unecclesiastical, was Archbishop Stone, and he lived in " Polish magnificence." At table, " the rake took the place of the Archbishop." He was appointed when still quite young, and had charming manners, a handsome person, and before a Viceroy came over, Archbishop Stone was solemnly consulted on the wines to be purchased for the Viceregal household. He gave his opinion with censorious authority, on a matter of importance ; for a great deal of government was carried on by the help of choice vintages.

The house or palace in which archbishops entertained was replaced later by the King's Inns Library, after Stone's day ; but the street retained its splendour to the end of the century. In 1798 the fifteen houses were occupied by five peers, one peeress, one peer's son, one landlord member of parliament, a judge, a bishop, and two rectors. There were fitted in also one doctor and one publican. By 1910 ten of the houses were tenements ; Sisters of Charity had No. 12, where the " most gorgeous Lady Blessington " once received.

It is typical of the fate which has come on what was the centre of fashion.

Fashion spread from Henrietta Street, along the top of the slope, seawards. People had begun to desire a view and from Charlemont House one can see how fine the outlook was, over the city to the mountains. The line was carried further along the slope, by Gardiner's Row to Mountjoy Square— a line of splendid houses. These names keep the memory of Luke Gardiner, afterwards Lord Mountjoy, who was the chief designer and layer-out of all this quarter.

It was he who built Sackville Street, but not as we see it ; he began at the upper end, and laid out what was called Gardiner's Mall—now the wide space in front of the Gresham Hotel. But towards the river there was a continuous line of houses along the quay, in what is still called Bachelor's Walk. The decisive change took place when John Beresford, Chief Commissioner of Customs, settled to place the new Custom House half a mile further down the river, abandoning the old building, which was falling into ruin. The river up there was narrow and awkward for shipping ; foreign traffic complained of the inconvenience ; nothing over 300 tons could get an anchorage inside of the Liffey's bar. Part of the plan was the construction of a new bridge on the line between College Green and Sackville Street.

There is no doubt that Beresford was right.

Whether the finances of the time justified it or no, he added to the glory of Dublin by the Custom House, which was designed in obedience to his lordly ideas. But he and Gardiner were close allies and Dublin of that day protested loudly against burdening the city with expense for the profit of two individuals, since the values about Sackville Street would increase as the centre of commerce shifted down the river.

None the less, the thing was done. The Custom House began to be built. In 1782 the Commission set up by Parliament for widening the streets made a grant to continue Sackville Street to the river and link it with Westmoreland Street. So, with much pulling down of narrow ways on both sides, the passage was cleared and Westmoreland Street, itself impressively wide, leads over a bridge—now extended to the street's full breadth—to Dublin's great boulevard, forty yards wide and seven hundred long.

Dublin of to-day finds it hard to realise that this main artery did not always exist. But at the very time when Grattan was claiming the independence of Ireland, papers were full of angry protests that all this heavy outlay was to promote " the great business of visiting," carried on between the fine folks in Kildare Street and Merrion Square and Stephen's Green and the fine folks in Sackville Street and the quarters that were nearest the Rotunda.

THE REV. T. A. FINLAY, S.J.
By Leo Whelan, R.H.A

DR. DENIS COFFEY
By Sir William Orpen, R.A.

Yet nobody foresaw what was going to happen ; how the whole life of the wealthy community was going to drain away southward. I have given figures about Henrietta Street : the same process has been at work wherever modern offices or business premises have not taken the place of old dwellings. From the slope by Gardiner's Row and Mountjoy Square, streets lead down that are wide and stately in places, with fine ornamented fanlights on many doors—but it is not well to look inside the houses. Most of the ornament that could be removed has been taken away. Friends of mine decided to sell one of their north-side houses, an old inheritance, but neither of use nor of credit to them. Some time later the lady chanced to see two superb mantelpieces of the coloured inlay work introduced to Dublin by Bossi, an Italian, and asked their history. The dealer laughed. " Your ladyship ought to know them." They had come out of the old house and the price asked for them was much more than the freehold fetched.

The fine dwellings, of which Leinster House and Charlemont House are only the extreme examples, were for the most part the town houses of gentlefolk whose principal homes were in the country. They were attracted to Dublin by the presence of a parliament in which they or their relations had the right to speak or vote—and be rewarded for voting. After the Union—which came less than ten years after Carlisle Bridge was opened—these people continued to live in their Irish country seats, but town for them meant London, more and more ; and their Dublin houses passed to the professional classes, lawyers and doctors. These continued to be Dubliners, but the tide of fashion carried them across the river ; and all those streets on the north side which are to Dublin what Bloomsbury and Soho were to London of their time, slipped down and down in the scale of habitation and in the standard of living.

On the south side, extension of building was limited—happily limited—by two great open spaces. One was Stephen's Green, the old commonage. The other was the oblong tract, half a mile long and nearly as much across, which belonged to Trinity College.

The wide straight thoroughfare or boulevard that had been opened from the Rotunda to College Green had to narrow itself when it passed the front of Trinity College. That front had been built about 1760, replacing an older structure which had stood further back. Beyond it, Andrews, the Provost of Trinity, had caused to be built a residence for himself and his successors. Grafton Street begins in front of the wall which encloses the courtyard of the Provost's House ; it continues up towards Stephen's Green, Dublin's Bond Street, and, like Bond Street, it still keeps curves that remind us of the time when it was a muddy lane. But everything beyond Grafton Street is laid out in form severely rectilinear. All here is work of the eighteenth century. From the corner of the Provost's courtyard the wall of the College Park runs along, making one side of Nassau Street, which is roughly parallel with the nearer side of Stephen's Green. Two main streets, Dawson Street and Kildare Street, lead from the Green to Nassau Street. Cross streets, parallel to Nassau Street, connect them to Grafton Street and to each other.

All this is now Dublin's fashionable shopping centre. But in the eighteenth century it was a fashionable quarter to live in.

Dawson Street had been built soon after 1700. John Dawson, the respectable merchant whose speculation it was, built himself a very fine house in it ; so fine that in 1715 the Corporation bought it to be their Mansion House. The Oak Room was added for their uses, and is still available for many meetings of a reasonable size. The Round Room at the back, separate from the house itself, was constructed in a spasm of zeal when the Corporation wished to entertain George IV on his visit in 1821. Since that period of effusive loyalty, Convention after Convention of Nationalist Irishmen has been held there, and finally, at the end of 1918, when Nationalist Ireland went Republican, the elected members met in the Mansion House as the first Republican Dáil.

Meanwhile a statue of George II remained in

the garden, not wholly unmolested ; it was removed prudently to the rear and is, as I write, on its way to a more congenial home in Birmingham.

In George I's reign there was no Dublin at all beyond Dawson Street. Stephen's Green, west of it, was surrounded probably with buildings of no very distinguished type. But when the Earl of Kildare announced in 1740 that he was going to build a new mansion where Kildare Street now is, people asked whether it would not be lonely to live so far out. " Where I go, they will follow," said the Geraldine, fully conscious of his import- ance as the twentieth earl of Kildare. Then almost as soon as the house was finished, he was raised to the Dukedom of Leinster—head and front of the Irish peerage.

Leinster House was the first private mansion built of stone in Dublin on that side. Tyrone House, on the north side of Marlborough Street, had already set the example.

People did follow where the Geraldine led. Kildare Street came into being ; then, beyond Leinster House and Leinster Lawn (the noble garden space which the Duke reserved to himself on the further side), Merrion Square was planned, of the most spacious dimensions.

One could not say that this quarter was more fashionable than Rutland Square and the streets about it ; but it certainly ranked equal. Take, for instance, Upper Merrion Street—which continues past the National Gallery and Leinster Lawn. No. 24 was built in 1760 ; in 1769 Lord Mornington took a lease of it and his son, Arthur Wellesley, later the Duke of Wellington, was born there in November of that year. After Mornington, Lord Cloncurry had it, a liberal-minded peer whose liberalism carried him to be suspected in some quarters and respected in others. (His granddaughter, the Hon. Emily Lawless, was a staunch Unionist who wrote the best rebel poetry of her time in a volume called *The Wild Geese*.) But after Cloncurry, Lord Castlereagh had the house from 1799 to 1801, the years in which he was directing the bribery that carried the Act of Union.

Yet the real reason why Castlereagh was able to bribe a parliament of Irish landlords into voting for their own suppression was the fear lest a reform movement might give power to the Catholic tenantry, and the landlords lose the lands which had been confiscated from Catholics.

To-day No. 24 is the seat of the Irish Land Commission which, for the last forty years, has been superintending the gradual transfer of all Irish land from the landlord to the tenant ; and the Acts under which it worked were passed by the Parliament of the United Kingdom. This does not mean that the English Parliament passed them voluntarily ; they were the next concessions made to the long-drawn-out Irish revolution after the first point, Catholic emancipation, had been gained.

But the wheel has come full circle. Leinster House, the centre of that old landed aristocracy, is now the seat of an Irish parliament in which scarcely one man sits who is descended from the old landlord class. Irish landlords judged badly for their descendants and for Ireland when they let themselves be bought.

After that transaction, the landed aristocracy ceased to have town houses in Dublin ; but there were still rich men to take their places. English rule kept up an English standard of salaries for Irish judges ; Dublin medicine contrived also to maintain something like London charges.

John Gamble, himself a doctor, writing in 1811, a " Sketch of Irish History and Manners," says of Dublin : " The streets are wide and commodious, the houses uniform, lofty and elegant, nor do I know any square in London that equals Merrion Square for beauty and uniformity of appearance. Dublin physicians have thrown aside the grave airs and formal manners, with the large wigs and gold-headed canes ; they have a candour and openness of address far superior to their London brethren. The truth is, a physician here is almost at the pinnacle of greatness ; there are few resident nobility and gentry here since the Union, and the professors of law and medicine may be said to furnish the aristocracy of the place."

There was still lavish hospitality and intellectual distinction. For instance, No. 1 Merrion Square, the first house as you continue from Clare Street, was the abode of Robert Day, a lifelong friend of Grattan. Day arrived at a judgeship and lived long and happily. He was succeeded in the house by a brilliant eye-surgeon, Sir William Wilde, famous as an antiquarian. Lady Wilde, writing under the name " Speranza," was one of the poets of *The Nation* newspaper in the forties. Their son was Oscar Wilde, educated in the Dublin High School and at Trinity College, before he went to Oxford and started the " aesthetic " craze there. Grattan must have dined a score of times in No. 1 Merrion Square. Yet to-day probably more people will be interested in the house for the sake of one of those Irish writers who have written all the best English comedies from Congreve onwards.

Or again, Ely Place, which continues the line of Upper Merrion Street, is full of interest. No. 8 was Ely House, and here up till twenty years ago a Dublin surgeon, Sir Thornley Stoker, maintained one of these mansions in its old splendour, furnishing it with choice examples of all that belonged to the period and matched the splendid plaster work and marble mantelpieces. These which are part of the structure at least survive, and it may be possible to get leave to see the interior, occupied by the National Health Association, founded by Lady Aberdeen. No. 6 in the same street is more typical of what has generally happened : a government office occupies what was the residence of John FitzGibbon, Lord Clare. Allied with Grattan and the rest to recover freedom for the Irish Parliament, he turned against them, and as Lord Chancellor did more than any other man to ruin Ireland. But you can see the staircase of white stone, curving with the sweep of a bird's wing, which he had built to lead to a banqueting room, forty feet long. You can also see his state carriage in the National Museum.

Ely Place is divided from Upper Merrion Street by the beginning of Baggot Street—a thoroughfare running southward from Stephen's Green. But the main route for traffic towards Dún Laoghaire is the line of Nassau Street and Merrion Square through Mount Street to the Grand Canal. This canal marks the limit of Georgian Dublin. If you follow it westwards from Mount Street to where Baggot Street crosses it, and then to Leeson Street Bridge, you will have on your right very little but fine Georgian houses and streets, spreading out from Merrion Square and from the less imposing, but very charming, Fitzwilliam Square. All this was built in the last quarter of the eighteenth century, or first quarter of the nineteenth. In 1750 there was nothing beyond Stephen's Green. One of the most famous examples of early Georgian building is Mespil House, which stands beyond the canal ; there are letters from its prosperous owner talking

of his "country retreat." Only two or three
detached houses stood then along the road which
led to it from Stephen's Green—the present Lower
Leeson Street. Towards the village of Donnybrook
and its bridge over the river Dodder, the road ran
through open country.

This roadway, passing from the south-west
corner of Stephen's Green along Lower Leeson
Street to the canal, and then by Upper Leeson
Street and Morehampton Road to Donnybrook,
keeps the curving lines which tell of antiquity :
and indeed before ever Dublin was a city, this was
one of the main roads of Ireland, leading from
the Hurdle Ford southward to Wicklow. One of
the great public places of hospitality was fixed on
it : not where it crossed the Liffey, but by the
banks of the little Dodder. A very ancient Gaelic
poem tells how Conary, High King of Ireland,
lodged here with his retinue and was taken unawares
by pirates from oversea, guided by Irish exiles.
"The Sack of Da Derga's Hostel," considered as
a saga, brings in too much of the supernatural
to be easily appreciated by our age. Yet the same
is true of the better known epics whose action
centres about Tara or about Armagh ; and there
is no more doubt but that Da Derga's hostel existed
here as a public institution than that Tara and
Ardmacha were seats of native sovereignty.

As happened in other places, this ancient meeting
place remained the place for a traditional assembly

and Donnybrook Fair lasted till a century ago. It had a great name for diversions, not always refined. " Two men will grin upon the common against two women for three rolls of tobacco. Proper scaffolds will be erected, to convenience spectators." But the fair was in some ways too popular ; too many heads were broken there ; and the Corporation had it put down—leaving only stories about it like that of the man who succumbed to the stroke of a shillelagh. Medical evidence was given that his cranium was of less than usual thickness ; and the verdict was, a man with a skull like that had no right to go to Donnybrook Fair.

Another Georgian street leads out of Stephen's Green and continues the same type of building westwards. This is Harcourt Street, named after the Viceroy who was in office when Grattan entered Parliament. Several useful hotels now make it well known to strangers. One house, No. 39, for several years held the Municipal Gallery : its first occupant was Scott, Lord Clonmell, a contemporary and opponent of Grattan's ; a duellist and a bully, of whom it might have been said, as was said of Lord Norbury, that he " shot himself up " to preferment. At the other end of the street is the High School where Oscar Wilde and his brother William were educated.

Harcourt Street is now the main track to

Rathmines and Rathfarnham, suburbs that lie towards the mountains, not along the coast. But it was not the road there for old Dublin. That started from Dame Street, probably nearer the Castle than the point where South Great George's Street now carries the tramline ; it certainly entered that narrow twisting thoroughfare which winds through parts of Dublin much older than Grattan's day. South Great George's Street and its continuation, Aungier Street, are narrow enough, many streets and lanes still narrower give on to them, leading towards St. Patrick's—where was the weavers' quarter—or on the other side towards Stephen's Green. In the days when guerilla war raged in Dublin, British armoured lorries used to call this way " the passage of the Dardanelles."

It widens out before this tramline meets the other line up Harcourt Street at the South Circular Road. Dublin of Grattan's day decided to put a girdle round itself, and they made this broad track, inside of the canal, which also they had engineered. From the Grand Canal Dock near the harbour of Ring's End, where the Dodder falls into the Liffey, the Circular Road ran roughly parallel to the canal as far as Leeson Street. Here, diverging from the canal, it crossed the road to Rathmines, and beyond that the road to Harold's Cross, and so swung round north-west, beyond Kilmainham, to the Liffey. On the other side, the North Circular Road cut across a corner of the

Phoenix Park, and ran in a great curve behind the quarter which was still spreading about Rutland Square, and so came down, beyond what is now Amiens Street Station, to the starting place of the Royal Canal that was meant to serve the northern half of Ireland.

If you follow the street by which the Rathmines tram continues from the Circular Road, you will notice a Georgian building facing the canal lock by the Portobello' Bridge. It is a hospital now ; but it was built for a hotel, at which passengers reaching the canal harbour (ambitiously styled Portobello) should find entertainment ready. And although for a hundred years past the canal has carried nothing but barges (laden chiefly, outward, with Guinness, and inward with turf from the great central Bog of Allen) for fifty years or more it was a substitute for coach roads. Houseboats, such as you may see at Henley or at Oxford, plied on it, drawn by a pair of horses. There was better shelter there than in a coach, food was provided, not without drink ; it was smooth running and if they kept their scheduled time the journey of seventy-eight miles was done in eleven hours.

That journey is not often made now, except by the people of the barges ; but I once, by special privilege, helped to take a boat through, and found myself in a region far less known than Connemara or Donegal. But the most surprising thing in that voyage was to see, about thirty miles from Dublin, a replica of this Portobello building rising from the bank. It had been another hotel, placed where the southward branch from Athy joined the main canal. When we reached Shannon Harbour, a little above Banagher, there was a third of these edifices—as I ought to have known, for Lever, in his *Jack Hinton*, describes the journey down by canal boat and there is a final scene in this hotel.

Lever made fun out of it all, as was his fashion : but a certain Dr. Johnson (not Samuel) has left a more steady-going account of this way of travel. It need not have been specially slow for, as my companion and I found when a motor failed us, a man can haul a seafaring boat at a good walking pace : and one stretch between lock and lock is almost thirty miles. We found proud memories of the haste that was used at every lock to let the " fly-boat " through and tackle up the horses for the next run. A picture of the period shows the fly-boat coming in with colours streaming to Portobello harbour.

Beyond the canal all is Dublin of the nineteenth century. Dr. Chart observes that from 1860 onwards, when a tram service was started, citizens made haste to get themselves homes away from the low-lying city. Rathmines and its neighbouring suburbs acquired a name for gentility ; there was even a " Rathmines accent "—with the " th " well marked. (But common people, as usual, preserve the proper pronunciation and say Ra'mines ; the

77

" th " in Rath, a fort, is silent in Gaelic). Rathmines and its adjacent suburbs, Palmerston and
Rathgar, which used to make a separate muni-
cipality of 70,000 people, are now aware that
fashion tends rather to the new suburbs that have
grown up beyond the Dodder along the line to
Dunleary. But there are pleasant streets out here,
well planted, and hospitable houses. If ever
Dublin extends the laudable practice of setting
up memorial plates, one should go on 5 Castlewood
Avenue (where the No. 18 tram branches off the
main Rathmines line, connecting to Pembroke
Road). Here William Osborne, the animal painter,
and his son Walter, worked and died—the son unhappily cut off in the full strength of his manhood
and his delightful talent. Another should be on
17 Rathgar Avenue ; here George Russell ("Æ")
used every Sunday evening to be at home for those
who came to listen to his outpouring of wise and
beautiful discourse. Yet perhaps memory of that
shaggy sage is even more closely associated with
84 Merrion Square, "The Plunkett House"—given
by Sir Horace Plunkett's many admirers to be a
centre of that great gentleman's beneficent activities.

Horace Plunkett's work for co-operation in agriculture and Plunkett's personality found admirers
all over the English-speaking world : Theodore
Roosevelt was among the chief of them. But the
most important action of his life was done when he
took a young poet and mystic out of a cashier's

office and set him to preach agricultural economics
to the people of Ireland. Nobody can separate
the memories of these two Irishmen, unlike in all
except in their great goodness and nobility. For
twenty years at least, whoever came to Dublin to
inform himself about Ireland came to Plunkett ;
and whoever came to Plunkett was sent to see "Æ"
in that crowded room at the top of The Plunkett
House, where the bearded propagandist sat among
a jumble of books and papers, between walls decor-
ated by images of strange visionary shapes. What
positive result came of it all, would not be easy to
define ; but no one could come in contact with
" Æ " and not be better for it. He survives not
by his own work alone, but by the impress of his
personality on what was written in Ireland during
more than a full generation.

And since I talk of memorial tablets, there should
be another—on the wall of 4 Upper Ely Place : one
of what the Georgian Society calls " a group of
uninteresting houses " in that fine Georgian street.
Uninteresting as architecture ; but here George
Moore wrote the books, *Ave*, *Vale* and *Salve*, which
many of us think to be his best work, and which
in any case keep a picture of Dubliners in the
beginning of the twentieth century, when the
literary revival ran strong. The best that was
in those books, the best that was in George Moore,
will be found in the impression that they preserve
of " Æ's " personality.

CHAPTER VI

HAVING sketched the growth and the general lay-out of Dublin, I go on to describe the buildings in which the capital of Ireland has its central activities, and the associations which they recall.

Eire, formerly the Irish Free State, is a democracy of the extreme type. All men and women over twenty-one are electors of the parliament to which the Government is responsible and which chooses the Government. This democratic parliament is housed in the mansion built by the greatest aristocrat in an aristocratic society. The twentieth Earl of Kildare, who became the first Duke of Leinster, was the direct descendant of the sixth earl, concerning whom it was reported to Henry VII of England that all Ireland could not rule the Earl of Kildare. Then, said Henry, let the Earl of Kildare rule all Ireland. And he did. His son, the seventh earl, did the same. But Henry VIII and Cardinal Wolsey decided to end this pre-eminence; Earl Garrett was summoned to England and thrown into the Tower. His son, known as Silken Thomas, went into rebellion and the English Government saw their

DR. SALMON
By Benjamin Constant.

ST. PATRICK'S CATHEDRAL—SOUTH SIDE

chance. The Geraldine castle at Maynooth, half a day's ride from Dublin, was reduced by artillery, Silken Thomas was executed ; and to make a clean end, every male of the Geraldine house that the English power could reach was put to death also. Yet the youngest son, according to the usage of time, was in fosterage with a friendly household ; all Ireland protected him. O'Donnells in the north, O'Briens in the south, passed him from one to the other till he escaped to the Continent and there grew up.

Under Elizabeth he was allowed to return, lived at the English Court with his honours restored, and joined the English Church. Succeeding earls kept out of trouble through the seventeenth century, and possessions accumulated. In 1739 the twentieth Earl acquired land beside Maynooth and built there his great palace, Carton. When that was done, the same architect, Cassels, was employed to build the Dublin mansion.

In Grattan's day, the second Duke was head and front of all ceremonies in Dublin ; and he identified himself in all ways with Ireland. On March 16th, 1778, on the eve of St. Patrick's day, there was a fashionable masquerade at the Assembly Rooms in Fishamble Street and the Duke appeared disguised as an orange seller ; but there was great applause when midnight struck and the oranges in the baskets were exchanged for shamrocks, and offered to all the company. Again, in 1779, on November 6th, when the Volunteers paraded in College Green with a motto on their cannon " Free Trade or This," three volleys of musketry were fired. " When after the third volley the Duke of Leinster flung up his hat in a huzza, there was not a covered head to be seen in all that vast assemblage," says the *Freeman's Journal*.

The Duke remained constant to Ireland's claims for independence : but his younger brother, Lord Edward Fitzgerald, went much further, in the years when revolution in France spread a ferment of new ideas. Lord Edward not only went to France in early days of the Revolution, but found a charming bride there, Pamela, daughter of Madame de Genlis, and, it is believed, of Philippe Egalité. In Ireland he joined the United Irishmen, and when this organisation was driven to despair of reform by constitutional means, Lord Edward was chosen as their military head—partly because he was a soldier who had seen service, but even more because of the traditional leadership of the Geraldines.

The plans for rising were betrayed : Lord Edward escaped arrest for a few days, but was tracked down to a house in Thomas Street, part of the old High Street leading from the Castle to St. James's Gate, and there was mortally wounded in a desperate resistance. A tablet marks the house.

For the rebel's sake Ireland has always felt kindness towards Leinster House and the whole Geraldine name : though indeed Lord Edward himself, who had been caught with Rousseau's notions of simple living, thought Leinster House gloomy, and much preferred a cottage with his Pamela to those suites of stately reception-rooms.

After the Union the Duke, like other Irish nobles, found little use for a Dublin abode in Dublin, and he sold Leinster House to the Royal Dublin Society. This organisation was founded in 1731 for the encouragement of agriculture and industry and did much good work by offering premiums and the like. Its library was nobly housed in the great room which runs the whole depth of the building, from the courtyard opening off Kildare Street to the windows that look out on Leinster Lawn. In course of years the Society added to the building a semi-circular theatre, with two galleries, in which concerts could be given.

As the work developed, it began to organise competitive shows of the finest horses and cattle that Ireland could produce, and for this purpose the Society acquired a large extent of land at Ballsbridge just across the Dodder, on the main road to what was then called Kingstown. Since Ireland, by its natural advantages and a widespread instinct among its people, led the world in breeding bloodstock, the annual Horse Show, held in the first week of August, became a great event in the social year. Handsome buildings were erected for the use of members and their committees connected with this side of the Society's work.

Meantime another movement had led to the creation of other buildings near Leinster House. After Mr. Gladstone's second Home Rule Bill had been defeated, a Conservative government came into power and was inclined to " kill Home Rule with kindness." It was decided to set up a Department of Agriculture and Industry and Sir Horace Plunkett was put at the head of it, with large funds. Under his auspices, offices on a splendid scale were built in Upper Merrion Street on the side adjoining Leinster Lawn. Besides these other buildings were constructed to house a new College of Science. These were hardly completed when the European war brought in its train the beginnings of the Irish revolution.

In December, 1921, after long negotiation, the Treaty was signed which recognised the Irish Free State as having rights equal to those possessed by the Dominion of Canada. It had to be accepted or rejected by the only body which could speak for Ireland—the members chosen at the last general election for Parliament, after the Armistice in December, 1918. But this parliament had no place appropriated to its meeting : debates on the Treaty were held in the hall of University College. There the Treaty was accepted by a narrow margin of seven votes, and the minority refused to be bound by the decision. The majority, led by Griffith and Collins, were left to bring the new State into being.

Part of the compact was that a fresh parliament should be elected which should draft a Constitution for the Free State. But before the date of the elections was fixed, revolt had begun : when they were over, civil war broke out. Griffith dropped dead; ten days later Collins was killed in a skirmish, and a group of young men, with Mr. Cosgrave as President, became the government. They held Dublin, but there was still sporadic rifle fire in the streets. They needed offices for their work and a place of meeting for the parliament. Too much unpopularity was attached to the name for Dublin Castle to be a possible centre. In these straits, they utilised for offices the Department of Agriculture and the buildings in contact with it which belonged to the College of Science. These reached so far back that they almost touched the west wing of Leinster House. Leinster House was accordingly borrowed from the Royal Dublin Society and its theatre became the meeting place of Ireland's new parliament—Dáil Eireann.

Through the whole of that autumn and winter and the following spring this group of buildings was held as a fortified enclosure. Every access was guarded by men with revolvers in hand. A covered way connected the offices in Merrion Street to the parliament house. By the time peace was established (among smouldering embers), the Dáil had become used to its abode. The Society, which had accommodated itself in the premises at Ballsbridge, consented to a sale ; and in this haphazard way the seat of Ireland's legislature and of its central government offices came to be determined.

When a Senate was chosen under the new constitution, it had to be housed for some years in an apartment belonging to the National Museum of Antiquities ; cases full of flint arrowheads and such like relics of primitive man were stored along the lobbies in Leinster House, among which members of the Dáil went about their various occupations. Later this was remedied, the flint implements went back to the Museum, and the Senate moved to fine quarters on the upper floor, in what was said to be the Duke's dining-room. It has at all events the recess for a musician's gallery in which the Chairman now presides, and the whole apartment is a magnificent example of eighteenth-century plaster work and marble work, used with the finest sense of proportion.

The library is now reserved for the use of members, though a visitor can probably get leave to glance in. The Chamber itself is work of the nineteenth century—an amphitheatre, like that where the Deputies sit in Paris, not an oblong, as at Westminster. There are five tiers of seats ; the Speaker faces the semi-circle ; Government

benches are on his left, with Ministers in the lowest
tier ; Opposition faces them and the middle of the
curve is divided between Labour members, who rub
shoulders with government supporters and Independents, next to the party which does not ask for
a Republic. A gallery behind the upper rows
of seats is reserved for the coming and going of
members who, while in it, are technically outside
the House. Above, an upper gallery accommodates
perhaps a hundred of the public—who do not
always refrain from applause.

It would be inexact to say that debates in the
Dáil have raised Ireland's reputation for eloquence.
That however can look after itself. But within
five years a native Irish administration had
knocked the bottom out of an often repeated theory
that Irishmen were useful for administration everywhere but at home. Mr. Cosgrave's government
had to bring order out of chaos ; they restored
order, and while they did it, reconstituted the whole
system of roads, and by a bold undertaking brought
electric power in reach of every corner of the Free
State. I later read with grim amusement the
speech of a Conservative Minister at Westminster
asking why the British Government could not do
for the British cattle industry what had been done
in Ireland by Mr. Patrick Hogan, whom Sir
Horace Plunkett described as the best Minister
for Agriculture in Europe.—A motor accident ended
that brilliant young man. His contemporary,

Kevin O'Higgins, who came to a more tragic and disastrous end, was probably the ablest man in the Dáil; no orator, but his trenchant intelligence made deep impression when statesmen of the British Empire met in Conference. These men contributed something worth more than eloquence; and since they are dead, we may praise them freely. It is only just to say also that when Mr. de Valera has addressed the League of Nations at Geneva, he has done credit to the parliament and the nation for whom he spoke.

But how the Irish Parliament which ended in Grattan's day would have stared, if in a vision it could have seen its successor! No Catholic was allowed to sit in that assembly of Protestant landlords and lawyers. In Dáil Eireann no bar exists against any sect; Mr. Blythe, Minister of Finance, was an Ulster Presbyterian—though a vehement Gaelic Leaguer and deep in the war against England. Other Protestants sat there, three of them representing Trinity College; another, who had earned the Military Cross as an officer in the British army, was returned at the head of the poll for Donegal—a most Catholic county. But the assembly was nine-tenths of it Catholic, because, broadly speaking, Protestants as a class had been opposed to self-government. Of the old landlord class there was only one whose forefathers had sat in an Irish Parliament. This was Captain Bryan Cooper, whose great grandfather, Joshua Cooper

of Markree, in County Sligo, voted sometimes
with Grattan, sometimes against him. Bryan
Cooper had been in the House of Commons as a
Unionist member ; he was returned to the Dáil
as an Independent, but generally supported
Mr. Cosgrave. One may safely say that there
was no man more generally liked in the assembly
or more regretted when he died.

The Senate as at first constituted was an interesting body. Half of the sixty men were elected by
a general vote of the democracy, and no very
significant name appeared among these. But
Mr. Cosgrave had the right to name half, and
among his nominees was a very able lawyer,
Lord Glenavy, who had been (as Sir James
Campbell) very prominent against Home Rule.
But the Senate chose him for its chairman, knowing
his ability. A more picturesque figure was W. B.
Yeats, who used his position there more especially
to protest against the establishment of a
censorship. George Russell was nominated, but
refused to serve. But Letters continued to be
represented by Dr. Oliver Gogarty, a distinguished
throat specialist, yet far better known as a wit
and poet. While that Senate lasted his speeches
were its delight. As a whole, debating there was
much superior to that in the Dáil. What the new
Senate may contribute is as yet only matter for
guess work.

On the whole, most of us who are Nationalists

would sooner see the Irish Government and the Irish Parliament judged by their work than by their public displays in parliament. Yet no parliament is made till it has created a tradition, and a parliament in the making is always interesting. Those who get the opportunity to observe it should remember that it is the parliament of a nation not yet twenty years emerged from a violent revolution. In that revolution, the richer people and the more expensively educated were as a rule opposed to the popular side : naturally enough, the new government was formed without them. But it is to be hoped that the old landlord class is not lost for ever to the public service of Ireland. They are landlords no longer ; the soil of Ireland is not their inheritance. But they inherit much from the race of men who built so much of Dublin in a style of which Leinster House itself is only the extreme example—and who also, for that matter, were the chief promoters and directors of the Royal Dublin Society.

CHAPTER VII

DUBLIN SOCIETY

A GREAT deal has been said in this book and in scores of other books about the fine buildings and the notable museums which Dublin can show. But to my mind the real interest of Dublin does not lie in its brick and stone, or even in its historic treasures. It lies in the life of a capital which has been through extraordinary vicissitudes and has not yet fully emerged from the last of them.

Society in Dublin is known to us by three distinct phases or transformations—though of course they shade into each other. There was first that of the eighteenth century, clearly marked off at its end by the passing of the Union in 1800. For a marking date at the beginning, one may take Swift's coming over in 1699 as part of Lord Berkeley's train. It is through Swift's eyes that we have to see Dublin up till his death in 1745. The terrible Dean had a " terrible eye for rottenness " and what we see is no more flattering than Gulliver's vision of humanity. Nevertheless we find him about 1720 trying to persuade Pope to come over and live near him. Living, he urged, was cheap compared to London and there were half a dozen houses where Pope would find as good entertainment and as good tables as London could offer. Swift had a free foot in the Castle, he stormed and battered his way in there when he chose ; but the people with whom he lived were mostly clergy, of the more scholarly kind. One was Thomas Sheridan, grandfather of the dramatist whose comedies have never lost their hold on the stage ; and Thomas Sheridan had wit in plenty but little wisdom. Swift had got him intimate with the Lord Lieutenant, Carteret, himself a wit and scholar, and there were high hopes of promotion when Sheridan was asked to preach in the foremost pulpit of Cork city. But the preacher either forgot or did not know that it was the day of thanksgiving for George I's accession to the throne and gave out as his text " Sufficient unto the day is the evil thereof." It was reported to Dublin Castle as done of *malice prepense,* and though Carteret laughed, Sheridan's hash was settled.

All the Protestant gentry of Ireland were Hanoverian—for good reason : they thought that the Protestant ascendancy was tied up with the Hanoverian line. It used to be amusing in Dublin to count how many houses showed through the fanlight over their door a white horse—the Hanoverian emblem. Swift hated the Hanoverians with more than his usual power of detestation, and he never had a good word for the landlord class or the parliament in which they dominated.

Still, making every allowance, one has to think that the Dublin in which Swift lived had by no means so polished and ornate a society as flourished there in Grattan's day. The Viceroys came over only for short periods, and the social centre had frequent eclipses. It did not mend matters that one of the Lords Justices was always an archbishop and therefore always an Englishman : Swift, an Irishman who wanted to be a bishop and was not allowed to be one, regarded these with fury. In the last years of his life, Archbishop Boulter, as Lord Justice, lowered the value of the guinea by threepence. Out came a ballad, by Swift or by one of his allies, about " Pulling the Gold Down," and it was sung all through the streets. At a state dinner given by the Lord Mayor to the Lord Lieutenant, Boulter taxed Swift with stirring up the mob. " If I had held up my finger you would have been torn in pieces," said the Dean. Next day the bells of St. Patrick's were rung muffled, and a black flag flew from the steeple. Dublin thought at first that the Dean was dead but, learning the truth, went to its taverns and drank confusion to the enemies of Ireland. The Lord Lieutenant sent for Swift, who said he was too ill to come ; he was " sick of the country's disease."

One could best characterise Dublin by saying that it has always been a city of personalities— " great characthers." Swift is the first, and he

remains the most famous ; but he stood alone.
The age which followed had a whole crop of
them. " Buck " Whaley was a typical instance.
He backed himself to walk to Jerusalem and play
ball against the walls there, and won a deal of
money on accomplishing his bet. No. 86 in
Stephen's Green is the house where he lived and
we have his memoirs of the time. There was
certainly none of the English passion for avoiding
singularity about the Dublin of his days, and
though it was an aristocratic society, wit was a
passport. John Philpot Curran was a poor man's
son, but he made his way to the Bar, and there his
eloquence made him an amazing advocate ; his
wit made him courted everywhere. A dining club
was formed called the " Monks of St. Patrick."
Charlemont, Grattan and all the leading patriots
of the day belonged to it ; its original purpose was
to talk politics ; but they soon came to be known
as " The Monks of the Screw." Curran, as Grand
Prior, wrote their hilarious assembly song :

When St. Patrick our order erected
    And called us the Monks of the Screw,
Good rules he revealed to our abbot
    To guide us in what we should do.

My children be chaste, till you're tempted,
    When sober, be wise and discreet,
And humble your bodies with fasting
    Whene'er you've got nothing to eat.

94

The best of all the stories about Curran records his answer to a prosperous tobacconist, Lundy Foot, who had set up a carriage and wanted a motto suitable to his station. " Take ' *Quid rides ?* ' "—(Why laugh ?) said Curran—" then it can be read either in Latin or in English." But one of the best stories is of his defeat by a brother, who had a good share of Curran's wit, but not his application to business. Naturally the ne'er-do-well wanted frequent assistance from the prosperous orator, now living in 4 Ely Place, and promoted to a judgeship. Naturally there were often difficulties, and one morning the Master of the Rolls, issuing from his distinguished hall door saw a booth set up against the blank wall opposite No. 4. Above was the notice : " Curran, cobbler. If absent, apply over the way." Ely Place and Dublin must have laughed loud and long when they saw the booth, and louder when they saw it taken away.

The rich people of that day were notably generous to needy talent. Owenson, the actor, whose songs in English and in Irish were a great attraction at the Crow Street theatre, had a clever big-eyed daughter ; she was passed from one rich house to another as governess or companion until finally, under Lord Abercorn's roof, she met and married a physician of some distinction. The Abercorn influence soon saw to it that Mr. Morgan had a proper prefix to his name, and Sydney

Owenson became Lady Morgan, one of the cleverest among blue stockings.—Lord Moira, afterwards the Marquis of Hastings, a somewhat stiff-jointed nobleman, not only befriended Tom Moore, but made a friend of him. But indeed that son of a little grocer in Aungier Street (the house is marked by a tablet) was taken up by all Dublin society almost before he was out of his teens; and though most of his life was spent in England or on the Continent, his talent, his social charm and his singing gift were all formed in Dublin; and when he came back there famous, Dublin certainly regarded him as one of the most noted characters that Ireland had produced.

Yet Moore hardly belongs to the Dublin of the eighteenth century. Its social centre was the Castle, so to say officially, but it could do very well without the Castle's countenance. Leinster and Charlemont and a few others could set the fashion; and in fact the Viceroys had to fall in with it. Some of them fell in with it head over ears: Lord Townshend outdid the Irish in roystering conviviality; the Duke of Rutland's constitution could not stand the strain he put on it, and he died barely turned of thirty. Conolly, the richest commoner in Ireland, was brother-in-law to two Dukes, Leinster and Richmond; his great house, Castletown, near Celbridge, was a rival to Carton; and he was a chief patron of all the race meetings. But Dublin has no particular memory of these

THE OLD VICEREGAL LODGE

COMPETING ARMY TEAMS AT HORSE SHOW

Ireland in front followed by France, America, and The Netherlands.

men ; though the names of forgotten Viceroys
and Chief Secretaries marked the streets, as
at Carlisle Bridge and Eden Quay beside it.
Grattan and Flood are legends for their eloquence ;
echoes of it survive. But perhaps the man best
remembered of that day is Sir Boyle Roche, who
had been a gallant soldier and was never tired of
proclaiming how absurd it was that Catholics
should be legally forbidden to bear arms, when
illegally and surreptitiously hundreds of them had
proved themselves among the best fighting material
in British armies. Yet that is not why Sir Boyle
is remembered, but because of a frequent characteristic confusion in his speech. " Why should we
take all this pains to provide for posterity, Mr.
Speaker ? " he asked. " What has posterity ever
done for us ? " That is the perfect example of an
Irish bull which, as Mahaffy once said, is a sort
of confusion of thought often found among the
English—but with this difference : the Irish bull
is always pregnant.

After the Union, things changed. Socially, the
town grew less elegant. People complained that
they saw no one in the streets but shopkeepers.
We have all heard the same sort of talk a hundred
times since the revolution ; and yet Dublin in the
close of the nineteenth century had as much
distinction as Dublin in Grattan's day—though it
was of another kind : and I imagine that the end
of the twentieth will find Dublin essentially itself.

Through the nineteenth century the Castle still maintained the forms of a Court—though they were never very formal : Irish atmosphere modified them. Yet the presence of some rich English peer who, as a rule, spent much more than the lavish sum allotted to him by the State, kept up a standard of entertainment modelled on that of London. Salaries also, especially judicial salaries, were on an English scale—quite out of keeping with the need. A judge in England, accepting his dignified position and five thousand a year, generally accepted a smaller income than he had been earning : in Ireland, he got the security of quarterly payments and probably a large increase in money as well. Dublin society could not entertain on the Viceregal scale, as Leinster and Charlemont could have done, but it kept Dublin up to the standard of well-to-do London entertainment.

One powerful influence was added by the British army. Before the Union, Ireland theoretically had twelve thousand regular troops stationed there in permanence ; the numbers often fell to barely half of this. In the eighteenth century's most brilliant period, the regular army was quite eclipsed by the Volunteers, and one is not conscious of its officer class as a factor in society. But throughout the nineteenth century, under the Union, England used Ireland more and more as a camping ground and recruiting ground. Twenty-five thousand troops was the ordinary force ; and in a way it suited everybody. The British army liked Ireland, with its easy way of living, its sport so cheap to come by ; and Ireland (apart from politics) liked the British army—which indeed was very largely manned and officered by Irishmen. But the social traditions, the way of living in the officer class were set by the rich men in the regiment ; and the army, without meaning it, helped the Viceregal Court to keep Dublin society spending on the English scale. The Irish country gentry never wanted much prompting to spend beyond their means, and when they came to Dublin for the " Castle season," when presentations were made at Court and balls given, they spent freely in Dublin, which had as good tailors' shops, saddlers' shops and gunsmiths as could be found anywhere.

The population was growing fast and in 1840 Dublin was the capital for a matter of eight million people. And London was almost as far away from it as New York is to-day. There was a strong life in the city—a new stirring literary life, which one thing favoured. Before the Union, English copyright did not protect books in Ireland and Irish printers did a fine trade with pirated editions. Richardson, who wrote *Pamela* and *Clarissa Harlowe*, the most popular novels of their time, was a printer himself and the novels came from his own press ; but for all he could do, *Clarissa* and *Sir Charles Grandison* were on the Dublin market as soon as on the London one. It was the same about plays. Sheridan's *Duenna* was produced at Smock Alley piratically, without leave, and he appealed to the Irish Courts. But the Chancellor, Lord Lifford, an Englishman, said that the intellectual privileges of the Irish people must not be curtailed. Naturally Dublin publishers and managers preferred to take what they could get for nothing, and consequently, though Irish actors got their chance, Irish authors got none. But after the Union there was a flood of publishing in Dublin, and the *Dublin University Magazine* brought out many of Carleton's stories and launched Lever on the world as "Harry Lorrequer." Lever became its editor and for several years lived at Templeogue, on the outskirts of Dublin, in a big house shut in by a high wall, on the left of the roadway as you approach the little bridge on the Poddle. He kept open house and was as lavish and as deep in debt as any of his rattling heroes. He left Dublin to live on the Continent, but used to come back to his old haunts, and an old Fellow of Trinity remembered well how his friends helped him to avoid the unpleasantness of getting up early to catch the morning boat at Kingstown. They played whist through the night till it was time for breakfast.

Clarence Mangan, Dublin's equivalent for Edgar Allan Poe, was a characteristic figure of those times ; his "Dark Rosaleen" is one of Ireland's

scriptures : " The Nameless One " and " Gone
on the Wind " can hold their own with the few
things by which Poe is remembered for ever.
Like Poe, he was a fantastic and forlorn creature,
haunting the bookstalls in strange cloaked dress,
a rat of the libraries, and unhappily of the drinking
shops. But Burton's pencil drawing preserves
the beauty of his profile as it lay in death—a thing
that no one should miss in Dublin's National
Portrait Gallery. He was closely associated with
the writers of *The Nation*, Davis, Duffy and Mitchel
—that brilliant group.

But the figure that towered over Dublin in those
days was Daniel O'Connell, the Liberator, who
won Catholic Emancipation. Dublin and all
Ireland knew him as " the Counsellor," an advocate who claimed that he could drive a coach and
six through any Act of Parliament. He was a
" characther " who knew all the quirks and twists
of the Irish mind, for good and for bad. " Will
you swear the man was not dead, when the cross
was put to it ? " he stormed at a witness in the
case of a disputed testament, made by an illiterate.
" There was life in him when he signed it," the
witness persisted. " Will you, as you value your
immortal soul, swear on your Bible oath that
you did not put a live fly into the corpse's mouth
and a pen into his hand, and mark the paper with
it." The witness collapsed and admitted.

O'Connell was a type of which Grattan's Dublin

had no example : its great men were either of English ancestry or Anglo-Norman, and of the reformed religion. This huge Kerryman was Gael of the Gael, come from Catholic gentry who hung on precariously, sending the pick of their men abroad ; his uncle was the last colonel of the Irish Brigade under Louis XVI ; and Daniel O'Connell himself came back from a school at St. Omer in flight from the French Revolution. Physically and intellectually, he was titanic ; his voice could carry in all its modulations to the outskirts of vast assemblies in the open air ; and his oratory had magic in it that made Catholic Ireland, trampled down for a century, begin to rise and stand on its feet.

There was littleness mixed with his greatness, and in essence, like Grattan before him, he was too much a constitutionalist to carry through a revolution. His life and his influence went down together in the awful time of the famine which, with the frantic flight of emigrants that followed, brought down Ireland's numbers by two millions in ten years. With that ruin of the tenants went also ruin of the landlords : starving men, dead men, could pay no rents and mortgages were foreclosed. After 1850 Dublin was less and less a capital for the landed gentry, more and more a city owned by the prosperous *bourgeoisie*. Judges' salaries did not diminish, doctors kept up their fees ; the Viceregal Court went on ; it was an easy and still a lavish society.

As a young man I went to dine along with my father at the house of a judge, his college contemporary. There were half a dozen men of that standing, thirty to forty years my seniors; and the first thing that struck me was that I was drinking such wine as I had not met before : so I decided to conform myself to the example of my neighbour, the Fellow of Trinity who had played whist with Lever. Gradually then I became aware that one of the company, a little priest, was talking with a finish that matched the wine ; I can hear him saying, when after the champagne we came to the claret : " Bottled velvet with the odour of violets." It was Lafitte 1864, and in that house we drank nothing else except 1865 from that same august vineyard : and I never dined there without meeting the same priest, Father James Healy, of Bray. Dublin was full of his witticisms—perhaps the most characteristic was the explanation he gave of a projected tour to the East. " I thought I'd like to look in at Heliopolis and see if any of the family was left there." A Protestant rector of my acquaintance was calling on one of his parishioners when Father Healy came in. " Quite a canonical visit," he said, for both the divines had recently acquired the title. " A double-barrelled one," said the Protestant. " I'm glad the other barrel didn't go off first," was Father Healy's way of pushing the pun further. I saw him again and again hold the floor when there was a long table full of young people, and rattle off story after story in the broadest vein of Irish narrative. But that first evening, among men of his own standing, he took no more than his share of the talk, and a couple of stories that he told were in the fewest possible words, illustrating something that had been said, and getting their point just from an inflection of the voice, backed with some little movement of the hands.

The last time I saw him, he had stopped in Harcourt Street to watch a man persuading a drove of pigs down it. " Pigs are difficult to drive for one man, many, very," as Professor Tyrrell once put it into the idiom of Thucydides : and to see Father Healy's face as he watched was to watch a story in the making.

Tyrrell was another great Dublin character of that time and his rival, Mahaffy, even more so. but I must write of them elsewhere. Father Healy had a Protestant rival in Dean Dickinson, just as ingenious at punning. In the Protestant synod a tedious Mr. Brush was on his feet when Dean Dickinson interrupted, saying that " he did not think that Mr. Brush had been given any handle for such a sweeping assertion " ; and Mr. Brush could never get up again without being asked, where was his handle ?

It was an agreeable world, and some Viceroys made their Court very popular : Grafton Street would be full of gentlemen in pleasant country-looking tweeds and ladies with the country house stamp on them. They came up mostly to stay in old-fashioned family hotels and had their fill of fashionable entertainments of which the Viceregal party was the centre. Yet a large part of Dublin kept clear of the Viceregal Lodge and the Castle ; for from 1880 on, Ireland was in a fierce stage of revolution. Parnell's party was pledged against taking any office under a British government, and the government was prosecuting as criminals those leaders whom the mass of Ireland thought heroes. Broadly speaking, all Nationalists boycotted the Castle ; and a vast majority of Catholics were Nationalists.

It would not be easy to say whether Protestants deliberately avoided Catholics, or Catholics avoided Protestants, but in fact there was a deplorable separateness. The Protestants had the advantage of having authority on their side. One Catholic friend of mine said to me that he grew up believing society in Dublin to be entirely Catholic ; he realised now that when Dublin had a society, it was a Protestant society. He meant that society implies a certain organisation ; there was an organisation under the system of Viceroys, who might be Liberal or Conservative, but by law could not be Catholic. Under the Free State the old organisation has gone and nothing has taken its place.

Early in the twentieth century things had begun to change. There was a long period of Liberal rule, and Dublin Castle was, at least in theory, preparing for its own disappearance. Unionist gentry, and specially the landlord class, inclined to regard all Home Rulers as traitors and there was a social boycott of the Castle. Successive land laws had reduced the landlords' power and their wealth ; but up to 1906 they were quite ready to take a hand in whatever fun was going ; and under Lord Dudley, the last Unionist Viceroy of the old type, fun was plenty. When Lord and Lady Aberdeen came to the Castle, the Kildare Street Club, headquarters of the Unionist gentry, went into the sulks. And since most Nationalists would not go to the Castle or the Viceregal Lodge, the centre of Dublin society began to crumble.

Power began to shift also : many of the important posts in administration were held by Catholics ; and probably the balance of wealth began to change. I should say that the best dinners in Dublin at this time were given by a Catholic who was a member of Redmond's party : a man of the most scholarly culture, immensely read, but one who could never be induced to open his mouth in public. In private there were few better talkers than Lawrence Waldron, and no better host ; and his was one of the few houses where Catholic and Protestant met as a matter of course.

For the separation persisted. One of my Catholic friends used to go every Christmas to Switzerland for winter sports with a Dublin party nearly all Protestant ; and I asked him, " Do you see anything of these people at home? " " We just nod when we pass in the street," he said. It was really for the most part an affair of ruts : but ruts are very durable.

Then came the War and the troubles, and finally we emerged in a new world, extraordinarily like chaos. A crowd of untidy young men, with Michael Collins at their head, tumbled out of two taxis in the Castle Yard to take over. Lord Fitzalan met them, a lifelong Unionist, but a Catholic—the first Catholic Viceroy since the Battle of the Boyne. They recognised, I think, from his bearing the value for purposes of government of a certain dignity. But it was a year before there could be any escape from the atmosphere of hurry and makeshift that confused the outlines of more than one noble action and more than one high tragedy.

Then at last it was settled that in the Dominion of the Irish Free State the King's representative should be one chosen by the Dominion Government—" an old Irishman from the people." Through forty years Mr. Timothy Healy had been detested and admired ; admired in Ireland, then detested for the savagery of his attacks on Parnell ; detested in the House of Commons for his disregard of all its traditional decencies, then admired and enjoyed for his wit—especially when it was directed against his fellow Nationalists. He had reached at times the noblest pitch of eloquence and at times the lowest scurrility. But age had mellowed him and he had little occasion to forgive his enemies ; most of them were dead and he had helped to kill them.

Mr. Healy was a marked success as Governor-General ; he said many things that were for healing, few that opened sores. In many ways Ireland was proud to see him where he was, and certainly the Dublin that was Unionist welcomed him. But it was not possible for him to form a social centre and probably he never thought of it. After five years he was succeeded by a man much younger, whose life had been largely spent out of Ireland and whose part in Ireland had never been acutely controversial. Mr. James MacNeill had learned the art of ceremony in the Indian Civil Service, and he had a charming wife to help him. While they were at the Viceregal Lodge, society began with evident enjoyment to find a new centre. Protestant Unionist business men and professional men found much to approve in Mr. Cosgrave's government and nothing to disapprove in the Governor-General. But in 1931 Mr. de Valera came into power, determined that there should be no visible representative of the English throne in Ireland. The better the Lodge in

Phoenix Park served for social purposes, the worse it was from his point of view. He got rid of Mr. MacNeill and put in an amiable gentleman whose business was to keep completely out of sight, and who did it.

The society which had begun to form about the MacNeills had a feature quite new to us. Since Dublin was now the capital of a Free State, America set the example of sending a Minister and opening a Legation. France followed. Then the Vatican sent a Nuncio—the only Nuncio in any English-speaking land. Then Germany, then Italy raised their Consuls-General to the rank of Ministers : a diplomatic society was formed, and we found ourselves meeting at many entertainments not only French, Italian and German, but also agreeable and intelligent Czechs, Poles, Swiss, Belgians and Dutch, with their households. It made Dublin society immensely more interesting. The American Legation established in the old Chief Secretary's Lodge, a superb house in the Park, had all the advantage of priority : but France sent as a representative so genial and so hospitable a man that the big house which they acquired in Ailesbury Road, near Donnybrook, soon became an institution ; and M. Alphand's photograph appeared almost as often as the Lord Mayor's. We realised how great a tribute had been paid to Dublin when the Minister's next step was announced. M. Alphand was sent to Moscow to make the Franco-Soviet alliance—for good or bad, one of the most important things in European politics.

During the kind of interregnum in which the official head of the State was in eclipse, the Legations and Consulates have been a kind of framework about which Dublin society formed itself. It will, however, soon have to accept a new grouping, for under the new Constitution we are to have a President removed from political parties, and he is probably to reside where the American Legation was housed.

What exactly will happen there is not clear. But the Free State brought in very drastic sumptuary reforms. Salaries were lowered sharply from the English scale ; judges and departmental heads got incomes adapted to a society which lives no more expensively than those of the South German cities. Ministerial salaries were put almost absurdly low, in a zeal for democratic principle : Mr. de Valera, coming in, reduced them still further to £1,000 a year, free of income tax. These standards are now to be modified.

But there remains the question of ceremony. Mr. Cosgrave and his party accepted all the usual forms—including the symbolic top hat for attendance at a function. Mr. de Valera's group, coming in, were exceedingly anxious to be as little *bourgeoisie* as was possible, and the top hat was officially discarded. It became a matter of State concern

when their Ministry had to send representatives
to the important Dominion Conference at Ottawa
—where on certain occasions the top hat would be
de rigueur. We never fully ascertained whether
the Free State delegates conformed on this point,
but they were frequently twitted by their opponents
with having done so.

At all events, there is to be from 1938 onwards
a head of the Irish State, elected by the people,
and provided by the people with a very stately
residence and means to maintain it in Dublin.
This should in the nature of things become the
official centre of Dublin society, at which not only
Irishmen and women will presumably foregather
from time to time but will have along with them
representatives of nearly all civilised Europe. If
the Nationalist Irishman who is chosen to represent
Eire plays his part as easily and graciously as the
one who represented King George and is as well
supported by his consort, we may see Dublin
developing a new attraction for the Irish and for
all the world.

CHAPTER VIII

THE UNIVERSITIES

D<small>UBLIN</small> always had an advantage over cities which far outstripped it in numbers—Liverpool, Glasgow, Manchester and such like—because it was the seat of a Court, of an Administration, of a Judicature and of a Bar. It had advantage even over London, it was a university town. Edinburgh had the same privilege, and it is easy to see how much the university counted for in days when Edinburgh society was famous for its intellectual distinction. But Dublin's University was unique in type : partly attended by students living at home or in lodgings, as they do in Edinburgh and a score of other universities ; but partly a college where young men lived together within gates and under the sort of discipline which always leads to a good deal of cheerful disturbance.

Eighteenth-century newspapers are full of encounters between students and citizens, and college precincts were a sanctuary. In Goldsmith's day some bailiffs disregarded this, slipped in and arrested a student for debt ; whereupon the " college boys " turned out, seized the offender, dragged him and ducked him at the pump ; then, not being content to leave it at that, sallied forth

KUNO MEYER

By Augustus John, R.A.   National Gallery, Dublin.

MAHAFFY

By Orpen.   Municipal Gallery.

and tried to rush the " Black Dog " prison. There was even some shooting. Goldsmith, always eager to distinguish himself, was admonished as an active rioter.

In such encounters collegians do not appear to have gone armed, except with one special weapon. Each carried the key of his room, and these implements were of such proportion that, slipped into the foot of a stocking, or knotted in a handkerchief, great execution could be done with them. The whole pack stood together. In 1782 the lessee of Smock Alley had words with a fellow commoner trying to force his way on to the stage, and threw him out. Like a wise man, he wrote at once to the Provost, who issued a warning that if there was any attempt to raise a riot in the theatre any student concerned in it would be expelled from the University. At the same time, the Provost and Board expressed their determination to maintain and uphold on all occasions the rights and privileges of the students.

The Provost of that day was a leading member of the Irish government : nearly all the principal persons in Parliament (except, of course, the English Viceroy and Chief Secretary) had been educated in Trinity College, which had one advantage over Oxford and Cambridge. Its former students seldom lost sight of it ; at the Bar or in Parliament, they were constantly in touch with the life of their old university. College sent two representatives to the Irish House of Commons and to be one of them was always a special distinction. After the Union, when the Irish parliament ceased to exist, the university's two members sat at Westminster, and it became almost a routine procedure for an ambitious man to take this as a step on the way to law office ; and it cannot be denied that for fifty years before the Great War the representatives of Dublin University were much more widely known and more powerful than those of Oxford or Cambridge. The best known of them all, and the most powerful, was one of the last—Sir Edward Carson. He and his colleague, Sir James Campbell, were the two Dubliners who provided the Ulster opposition with brains and leadership.

So long as the government of Ireland remained English, and the Protestant ascendancy was maintained, Trinity had a great influence on Irish affairs. The Provost had official precedence under the Union like that given to the Speaker of the House of Commons. A succession of great judges, trained in Trinity, provided Ireland with Lord Chancellors. Some of them, like Michael Morris, the first Lord Killanin, were Catholics (though these could not be Chancellors). Catholics could be powerful if they were on the side of England, for " law and order " and against " criminal agitation."

But Trinity College was the nursing mother also

of a very different brood. When there was an Irish parliament, its patriots, Grattan, Hussey Burgh and their allies, were Trinity men. So were others who pushed the idea of patriotism to greater extremes. Trinity has always been loyalist, but among the busts ranged along its library is one of Theobald Wolfe Tone, who went singlehanded and without resources to France and brought into action a great expedition with Hoche at its head. England's luck at sea prevailed ; but Tone came near to altering the course of history. Three of the Emmet brothers were Trinity men, though Robert, the youngest, was expelled before he completed his course, for treasonable practices. Thomas Davis, chief inspirer of the Young Ireland movement, was a Trinity man ; so was Isaac Butt, who launched the phrase " Home Rule." Douglas Hyde, father of the Gaelic League, was contemporary in Trinity with many men who helped Yeats in the revival of Irish literature—notably T. W. Rolleston, whose poem on " The Dead at Clonmacnoise " is among the few entirely successful transpositions from Gaelic.

In the later movements of the struggle for Irish freedom, the student life of Dublin played a great part ; but it was not the student life of Trinity College. Dublin is now that exceptional thing, a city with two universities. The reason will be found in the history of Trinity College.

It was founded in the reign of Queen Elizabeth

and it was meant to educate people living in Ireland. But they must be educated according to the tenets of the Protestant religion. This was one important stronghold, finally established after the Battle of the Boyne.

From the Restoration on, when Dublin was really beginning to be a capital city, some very interesting people came to Trinity. Jonathan Swift was one ; so was Congreve, the dramatist, who had been a younger school-fellow of his at Kilkenny. Another of the same time was Berkeley, the philosopher. Swift, at least, had no affectionate memory of the place. The way of life in which young men live together closely in a community is apt to be uncomfortable for those who have less money than their neighbours, and there were rich men at Dublin as at Oxford and Cambridge. Swift was poor and proud, and he was unhappy. Goldsmith, after him, was even poorer, and he had none of Swift's power to protect himself ; he was very miserable there. Those who know the story of his life will think it a strange irony that his statue to-day should be one of two chosen by the University to set outside the noble front with which Trinity faces the world in College Green. Yet if Goldsmith could have known that he would stand there in company with Edmund Burke, it would have been consolation for all. They never knew each other in college, though Burke remembered Goldsmith—and he could only have remembered

him as an oddity, a butt and a failure. But later
they met as friends and equals in the most brilliant
society that England could show. To-day everybody knows Burke's name, yet it is Goldsmith
whose writings are the best remembered, perhaps
of any in that age ; and between the two statues,
in which Foley displayed his best genius, I think
the Goldsmith is the more sympathetic piece of
work. All through life this poor oddity was beset
by a sense of his own ugliness and insignificance ;
the sculptor has made the world see him for what
he was—a creature of gentleness who could teach
through laughter, and who was by nature " a
great lover of happy faces."

The roll of *alumni* is too long to review, but I
pick out a few. Tom Moore was here, a contemporary and friend of Robert Emmet ; as a
Catholic, he could not get a scholarship. That was
changed in the nineteenth century, and Catholics
came in considerable numbers, but their Church dis-
couraged this, thinking the atmosphere too Protestant to be safe for their faith. It is true also that
Trinity, as a whole, was against the Nationalist
side ; though as long as I can remember there
were always ardent and brilliant speakers on that
side in the Historical Society—a debating Club
whose record goes back to the time of Edmund
Burke. Some of them no doubt grew out of their
early opinions : one case was famous. In *The
Spirit of the Nation*, a collection of Young Ireland

verses, none was so popular as " Who Fears to Speak of Ninety-Eight ? " It was written by John Kells Ingram, then an undergraduate ; it was sung ten thousand times all over Ireland, long after Ingram was a Senior Fellow of the College and a staunch Unionist.

I have been writing of the collegians rather than the buildings. Trinity's façade is stately, the quadrangles which succeed each other within are dignified ; yet perhaps dignified is not quite the word to describe that one of them which lies off to the left as you pass the dining-hall and is known as Botany Bay. A little secluded from observation, it profits by the fact ; and I have known more than one Junior Dean (the academic official responsible for discipline) who thanked God when rain was seen falling heavy after dinner—a safe sign that there would be no bonfire in " the Bay."

In the space which you enter from the gateway are the essential public buildings, as well as ranges of living-rooms, opening off numbered staircases. The Chapel, on your left as you enter, faces the Examination Theatre—both of them places with many associations for those who are of the house. Outsiders, like the writer of this book, know better the dining-hall, with the long table on the dais set crosswise to the length. Here Fellows sit—and their fortunate guests. Other tables with benches on each side run down the length of the hall for the students. There, as in the English universities, the ritual of a Latin grace spoken by one of the scholars is duly maintained ; so is the tradition of a splendid hospitality. This, as in the Oxford and Cambridge Colleges, prolongs itself in a common-room to which, after dinner, the Fellows and their guests retire. Common-room and dining-room are hung with portraits of past worthies—the politicians, Grattan and others are in the dining-room ; the common-room is reserved for the more exclusively academic.

On occasion the dining-room becomes a theatre for set debate ; the chief societies, the " Historical " and the " Literary and Philosophic," hold their inaugural meetings here, at which the Provost presides, while an address is read by the auditor of the year. Chosen champions, brought from outside, say their say alternately upon it—with or without interruptions from the students massed in the body of the hall.

The ordinary weekly debates of the societies among their own members are held in a building in the second quadrangle, facing the Library. The debating rooms and club premises, corresponding to the Union at Oxford and at Cambridge, are modern—called the Graduates Memorial.

Beyond the Library Square is the New Square, given over entirely to living-rooms, and opening on to Trinity's most enviable possession—the College Park. No other college, no other university in these islands, or in Europe, has the match of it ;

a vast tract of green sward retained for the academic community at the very heart of a capital city. The green space runs parallel to the whole length of Nassau Street ; trees are planted along the low wall, considerately surmounted by a railing, so that passers-by in the tram-cars have the view. About a third of the length is reserved as the Fellows' Garden, pleasantly planted and gardened. The rest, during daylight, is open to the public and, as *Murray's Guide* says, " devoted to athletic purposes." I should think it was. Here is a cricket ground, on to which gentlemen of the College can step out straight from their rooms—not, as at Oxford, needing to travel a mile or more. And it is not only the College that profits : Dublin has been able to see there, off and on during all my life, all the most famous performers from W. G. Grace down. More than once some lusty man has lifted a ball to leg and broken a window in Nassau Street : indeed it sticks in my memory that in one of the first Australian teams, when Spofforth was dreaded as the demon bowler, a handsome giant, Bonner, hit a ball off some Irish bowler to a measured distance of 175 yards. But cricket is only one of the games : Rugby football is to be seen there at its very best. Only on rare occasions has a Dublin team been able to match the English universities on the cricket field, but at football they have always held their own.

In the summer term come what used to be one

of Dublin's great events—the College Races ; though perhaps in the new Dublin, where Trinity counts for less than it did, these athletic sports are not so well attended. One old feature of them has dropped almost out of memory—the walking races of seven miles, which champions used to cover, fair heel and toe, within the hour—pursuing their laborious way round and round the green space, while other events were being decided within it.

But any day in summer I know few things so agreeable in any great town as to enter Trinity by the Lincoln Place Gate, near Westland Row, and stroll along one of the shaded walks through the park, stopping to watch whatever game happens to be in progress ; and so out past the long colonnaded front of the Library and through the quadrangles to where close by the main gate women students in their rather becoming caps buzz like bees before a hive : for here is their common-room.—They have all to be outside gates by six o'clock, though.

The Provost's House, which continues the front of College facing Grafton Street is not generally accessible, but it is worth looking at as an example of how eighteenth-century Dublin thought that a gentleman should be handsomely housed. It was built under the direction of Provost Andrews, a man of taste ; he was the intimate friend of Peg Woffington, and some have suggested that he owed

his success in life to her influence. At all events
he did well by the College and his successors had
a noble abode : the state drawingroom on the first
floor is certainly the most magnificent apartment
in any Dublin house. Indeed, this is the only
great house of the eighteenth century still occupied
as it was meant to be occupied. There is, however,
to those who know, one lamentable symptom of
degeneracy. In the cellars, when I had the
opportunity to visit them, a few dozen bottles
lay forlornly among bins and vaults that would
have held a wine merchant's whole stock in trade.
And it is much to be feared that the cellars of the
community itself would show the same sad falling
away. Nevertheless, in Trinity College, as its
guests can testify, the old tradition of respect
for good claret is alive.

I have known half a dozen Provosts, and the
first of them, if he was not the greatest, certainly
presided over the most brilliant body of men that
Trinity ever knew, and by their general voice had
no superior among them. Dr. Salmon had a
European reputation in mathematics and then
went on to acquire another in theology. The
Provost's house keeps a portrait of him by Benjamin
Constant, in which the Frenchman has caught all
the character of a great untidy Irishman's very
untidy face. Like many men often immersed in
mathematical calculations, Salmon was indifferent
to considerations of dress ; I saw him once, when

he was Regius Professor of Theology, walking through the courts with his opposite number from Oxford ; what a pair ! the Oxford man, all straight up and down, with straight up and down side whiskers and these verticals crossed by a shining line of white collar ; Salmon, sprawling all ways, his whiskers like willows in a wind, his trousers like the legs of an elephant—but a genial impression of force and humour radiated from his whole bulk. There was a tale that he never looked at his clothes, but simply threw on what was laid out for him ; so one awful day, when his trousers were found lying on a chair, there was hue and cry for someone who had seen the Provost, and could confirm if he were more than usually noticeable. It was finally ascertained that by some unwonted freak he had of his own motion ordered a new pair of trousers and of his own motion put them on.

The group of Senior Fellows when he was Provost included Ingram, it included Abbott, both known to all specialists in their subjects ; it included Palmer, perhaps the finest latinist of his day, and Louis Claude Purser, who might have disputed the title with him, if he had ever in his life claimed anything against anybody. But above all, from the general public's point of view, it included Mahaffy and Tyrrell, leaders of opposite camps, both of them wits in the sense that the word was applied to Burke and to Dr. Johnson—

and indeed wits in any sense whatever. There was also Traill, whom nobody could have called a wit and who got the better of both of them, being made Provost in succession to Salmon.

Which of them Salmon would have preferred is not certain, he had sharpened his tongue often on both. The most famous instance is his reply to Mahaffy, who had been saying that he was only whipped once when he was a boy, " and that was for telling the truth." " It cured you, Mahaffy," said Salmon. These elders of the College Board, so far as I could make out, tore each other like dragons in the primeval slime. When Traill was chosen, he had to be sworn in by the Vice-Provost, Barlow, another original : and Barlow at that time was bedridden. So the Board went with the new Provost to where the Vice-Provost lived with his daughter (an admirable writer) and found the grey old man in a grey flannel nightshirt propped up in bed. Taking the statutes, he read out the Latin formula of appointment, then slammed the book together, saying, " And may God forgive me for what I am doing." Traill, who was slightly deaf (it was one of his resemblances to a rhinoceros) pressed forward and shook him warmly by the hand, " Thank you, thank you, my dear fellow "—and then in an aside, " I didn't quite catch what he was saying, but I suppose it was something civil."

The best praise that I ever heard of Traill

came from Mahaffy, who was bitterly angry—and no wonder—when he was passed over and Traill put in. But he said to me after a couple of years that he had never before seen the Board presided over with so much fairness and efficiency.

Mahaffy was, as I have said already, a famous "characther." Probably we did not know how great a man he was : a man of real learning, Henry Jackson, of Cambridge, once fell upon me for comparing him to a Cambridge don with whom he had some affinities. " The truth about Mahaffy," Jackson said, " is that he knows enough in three distinct lines to have a European reputation in each of them, and people do not believe this possible, so they think him superficial."

But one of the things that Mahaffy did not know was Irish, and he delighted to annoy the Irish people (a favourite pastime) by saying with his whole authority such things as : " That everything which has been written in Irish was either silly or indecent." But he knew a great deal about Ireland—anybody who consults the volumes of the Georgian Society for the study of the old Dublin will find characteristic examples of his witty learning : and somehow Ireland was proud of him. In 1917, when he was Provost, an Irish Convention was assembled to try to find some way of peaceable agreement, and it met in Trinity College—Mahaffy, of course, being a member. We were ardently desirous to be on our good behaviour and avoid causes of offence—all of us but Mahaffy. He let himself go when he felt like it. " Patriotism," he said, " is like alcohol ; taken in moderation it is healthful, stimulating, and agreeable ; taken in excess, it is a deadly poison, which corrupts the character." That is a mild example ; but one day, when he had been speaking his mind on the shortcomings of the Roman Catholic faith, I asked one of my friends how the mass of the assembly, mostly chairmen of County Councils, were standing it. The answer I got was, " Sure, it's only the Provost, and nobody minds him." He was a " characther," a chartered libertine.

I have left to the last the great storehouse of treasure for which Trinity College is most often visited—the Library, which has by Act of Parliament right to a copy of every book printed in the Three Kingdoms. They planned large in the eighteenth century, erecting a building ninety yards long to house a collection then of only some few thousand volumes. Now, like all other libraries, it is crowded out : the colonnade under it was long ago taken in and turned into a reading-room. To-day that no longer suffices and as a Memorial to those who served in the European war (how long a list !) another building has been added to the west, to give more space for readers and for books. Close to this is the statue of one by whom Trinity is widely known—W. E. H. Lecky, best of Irish historians for the period after Elizabeth.

After a stiff contest, the monopoly which lawyers had of Trinity's parliamentary representation was broken in his favour ; my father, then head of the Divinity School, was active in that good cause and never ceased to pride himself on one saying in an election speech. The lawyers, he said, promised much before they were elected ; but once in " they were like the statue of King William in College Green, with their face to the Castle and their back to the College." But Lecky in parliament was never a match for the lawyers ; no one was ever so academic, and his figure and movements as he stood to speak recalled those of that quaint and gentle creature, the giraffe.

In the magnificent columned room on the first floor are the show cases ; and everyone goes and should go there to look at the " Book of Kells "— most famous of all illuminated manuscripts. Skilled custodians show it and there is no use in describing the intricacy of its draughtsmanship or the brilliancy of colours laid on at least eleven centuries ago. But I would ask anyone to consider what effort of the brain as well as what skill of hand was needed. An artist before he begins must have the picture present before his mind—seen, as one put it to me, at the end of a very long funnel. How could any brain project in the abstract all that involution of the endless line which loops and curls itself in a thousand details of the pattern, so that even when it is there before us, no eye can follow its course?

It is the extreme type of what Irish skill could do when Ireland led the European world in the art of penmanship; but I find more interest in another example of that art—the "Book of Armagh": not a book really, but a library bound up together, all the work of one scribe, Ferdomnach. It contains one early manuscript of the Gospels of importance to Biblical scholars; but chiefly it contains the main documents for the life of St. Patrick, one of which is the saint's spiritual auto-biography—written in very bad Latin. This manuscript begins in the first person, "I, Patrick," and so on; and because at the end of it the transcriber noted, "Here ends the volume which Patrick wrote with his own hand," it was always believed that Armagh, chosen by Patrick to be the centre of the Irish Church, preserved the saint's actual autograph. The book was more than a book: it was a reliquary, and for all great occasions of treaty-making men took their oath on the *Canoinn Patraic*. Finally, in 1002, when Brian Boru, at last High King of Ireland, made a progress through all the country, he visited Armagh and there confirmed by decree the right of Armagh's cathedral to certain dues and properties. The decree was entered in his presence on a blank space in the sacred book. I give a photograph of the words—written down " in the sight of Brian

STAINED GLASS WINDOW FROM HARRY CLARKE STUDIO

These are two panels of the eight in the window designed for Geneva. The upper
illustrates Lady Gregory's *The Story Brought by Brigid* ; the lower, on the left,
Lennox Robinson's play *The Dreamer* ; on the right, Yeats's *Countess Cathleen.*

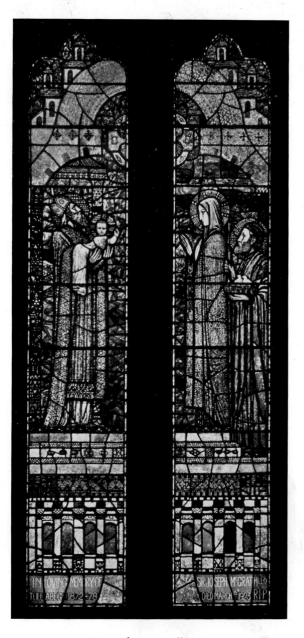

DESIGN FROM " AN TÚR GLOINE " BY M. HEALY FOR
THE MᶜGRATH MEMORIAL WINDOW AT CLONGOWES
(The Presentation in the Temple.)

Imperator of the Scoti," by his confessor and latinist, whose name also was given in a latinised form.

The book was not only treasured in Armagh, it was carried into battle as a luck-bringer : de Courcy, the Norman, captured it on one of these excursions, but restored it to Armagh, where it was guarded by a hereditary keeper or *Maor*. Centuries passed, the Reformation came, and conquest ; but the book was still with the family, now known as MacMyre—" Keeperson." In the days of the Popish plot and Titus Oates, evidence of conspiracy was sought against Oliver Plunket, Catholic Archbishop of Armagh ; the MacMyre of that day wanted blood-money, he pledged the book for five pounds to pay his expenses to London, and swore his lies there. The Archbishop was martyred ; but Florence MacMyre was not lucky with his pieces of silver : he rotted in a London jail. The book passed from hand to hand and finally, by a generous benefactor, was bought and brought to where all may see it : every stroke of the firm penmanship clear on the well-prepared sheepskins.

Yet I am writing of Trinity College, rather than of its treasures, which vary from prehistoric gold ornaments to a page of the Irish House of Commons roll, with signatures of those who voted for and against the Union. There are manuscripts too not less in importance than those of which I have written. But I must not catalogue : and a word has still to be said about the New Schools beside the Park, which I take to be the best building that nineteenth-century Dublin saw erected. The architects were Deane and Woodward ; Sir Thomas Deane, a Dublin man. They built also the Kildare Street Club, facing Nassau Street and the Park, at the corner of Kildare Street. In both buildings the influence of Ruskin's taste is seen departing from the severe eighteenth-century classicism towards an Italianised Gothic ; and a family of Dublin stonecutters was employed to carve borders of decoration along the structural lines. My father, then a Fellow of the College, remembered bringing them in plants to introduce into their detail, colts-foot leaves and the like. All the ornament on the College building is stylised treatment of growing flower and leaf ; but on the Kildare Street building they let a medieval fancy have scope, and you can see grotesque designs in relief of hounds after a hare, and of monkeys playing billiards.

The same architects were employed in Oxford to build the science schools opposite Keble College ; and they brought over the Dublin craftsmen to carry out the decoration. It can be seen there in long and delightful string courses, cleanly chipped. But the work stops : the design is not completed. What happened was that the O'Shea brothers painted the town of Oxford so often so red that the University authorities packed them back to

Dublin : but in the width of the British isles, no one could be found to finish their work.

The other university of which Dublin is the seat has a much shorter history. Various attempts were made in the nineteenth century to provide some institution that Catholics would accept : unfortunately what the Catholic conscience demanded, the British nonconformist conscience condemned as Popish. The Catholics raised funds privately, and Newman came over to be Rector of a Catholic university, with its habitation on the south side of Stephen's Green—including amongst other houses Buck Whaley's former abode. The institution languished : Parliament would not concede to it a charter with the right to confer degrees. Some men of mark were educated there : John Dillon, son of the 1848 leader, was preparing for a medical career and held a post as demonstrator in anatomy when the Parnellite movement called him into service, and his long career as a politician began. Meantime the Jesuit Order took over the enterprise and University College in Stephen's Green, with a medical school in Cecilia Street, continued to teach : from 1880 degrees were conferred by a body called the Royal University, which existed only to examine.

There was also the Queen's University, founded by Act of Parliament, with colleges in Belfast, Cork and Galway : but since all teaching of theology was prohibited by their statutes they were denounced by the Church as "the Godless colleges," and never filled up ; though many Catholics went to them, as they went also, and still go, to Trinity.

University College, under Jesuit direction, continued to turn out prize winners with the habitual efficiency of that Order ; but it turned out also men who were something more. T. M. Kettle was one of their products ; James Joyce (however they may regard the result) was another. These men passed through the college lecture room and its debating societies just before it was at last decided to make a National University, which should include University College, Cork and Galway. The whole was to be governed by a Senate sitting in Dublin ; but each college had considerable power to arrange its own affairs.

Cork and Galway were well provided with buildings ; University College was given a lump sum, and chose to acquire the great deserted building in Earlsfort Terrace which had been put up in 1853 to house an Exhibition. A very able architect, Mr. Butler—who became professor of Architecture in the University—rehandled the gaunt shell and provided it with the present dignified façade.

By 1911 the University was in working order and then came the European War. There was a Dublin Nationalist student population of about a thousand, and as all Europe knows, and Asia too, these are the choice seedbeds for revolution. In the first two years the revolutionary impulse was not marked, but after 1916 practically all the young men who had not gone to the War were in revolt. In scores of Catholic families, the elder brothers were with some Irish regiment ; the younger were training with the Volunteers to become part of the Irish Republican army. Kevin O'Higgins, for instance, had a brother serving in France.

Among the leaders in 1916 there was not a marked proportion of men from the University. Yet Pearse had lectured on Irish, and Thomas MacDonagh held a lectureship on Literature at University College, Dublin, and Mr. de Valera taught Mathematics at Blackrock to candidates for a degree. Eóin MacNeill, professor of Ancient Irish History, was at the head of the Volunteer movement.

But from 1919 onwards the University, which had been brought into existence by a government in which Mr. Lloyd George was a chief figure, was the very centre of resistance to Mr. Lloyd George's Government. De Valera, President of the Irish Republic, belonged to it ; and in the middle of the struggle, when Archbishop Walsh died, the University chose him for its Chancellor—professors and all associating in this protest against the Black and Tans. Richard Mulcahy, a medical student, was Chief of Staff to the unseen guerilla force, and hardly even Michael Collins had a bigger price on his head.

When the Free State was established, its ministry included Kevin O'Higgins and Patrick Hogan, who had been students after the University was established ; Patrick McGilligan, another brilliant man in Mr. Cosgrave's Ministry, was of the same flight. Eóin MacNeill, a much older man, was in the Ministry ; his sons, class-mates of O'Higgins and Hogan, were prominent in the army. John O'Sullivan, professor of History, a friend and contemporary of Kettle's, was Minister for Education.

He, however, had never been concerned with the revolution. Kettle, who also held a professorship, had answered Redmond's appeal and fell on the Somme, a few weeks after the Dublin rising—a grievous loss to the life of Ireland.

In Mr. de Valera's administration, the National University has been represented by the leader himself and by one of his colleagues, Mr. Little, who was an early propagandist of revolution in the University from 1914 on. It may be supposed that when Mr. de Valera by a new electoral law abolished direct university representation, he did not forget his party's interest. But whether the universities be represented in the Dáil as they were (having three members each in a house of 160) or send members only to the Senate, as is now

proposed, the National University has educated
and is now educating the men who rule and
will rule Ireland. Trinity's representatives sat in
the Dáil as Independents, not greatly affecting
or affected by either side, though respected by
both.

As to the National University's effect in other
ways, on general culture, it is too early to say
anything. When its doors were opened, Ireland
was full of political excitement over Home Rule
and the Ulster Volunteers ; then came the War,
the Revolution and the Civil War. University
life was not working normally for at least five or
six years after the Free State's beginning ; and
even now the political ferment is violent.

Student life has not yet had time to form its
own traditions. It is student life of the type found
at Edinburgh or Glasgow, not at Oxford or
Cambridge ; young men and young women living
in lodgings and meeting in the lecture rooms and
at organised games. It is no wonder that these
people should be jealous of Trinity when they
must go outside the city—to the grounds of a fine
old house on the road beyond Donnybrook—for
their playing fields.

There is, of course, a tradition which comes
down through University College, and one man
in particular may be said to represent it : Father
Tom Finlay of the Jesuit Order, who was professor
of Economics. No other man did so much to help

the spread of Horace Plunkett's movement. As a Protestant, a landlord, and a Unionist, Plunkett was suspect : Father Finlay brought him a first-rate brain in council and a most persuasive way of speech. Jesuits are not popular in the Protestant districts of Ulster, but when it was a question of establishing a creamery, he could go and talk to the farmers there. Once somebody shouted an interruption : " What about the Battle of the Boyne ? " Father Tom, in his suavest manner, said, " So far as I can learn, the Battle of the Boyne was a fight between an Englishman and a Dutchman, and neither of them cared two pins what happened to Ireland."

The University has in its council-room a portrait of Father Finlay by an Irish painter, Leo Whelan, which conveys all the strength of that finely moulded countenance, but does not suppress the twinkle in its deep-set eyes. In the same room is a portrait by Tuohy of Archbishop Walsh, the first Chancellor, not an impressive-looking person, even in his highly-coloured robes ; but very like the picture is to one of the ablest men who ever sat on a committee, extraordinarily quick and clear, and extraordinarily fair. There is also Orpen's portrait of Dr. Coffey, who was elected President of the College when the University was established, and since then has guided its affairs— some say, dictatorially. It was a quality which few had suspected him of possessing. But Orpen, working at his best, has brought out the force and the typically Milesian character of his academic countenance.

Some day the University will need and will acquire new buildings : it is cramped for space. But what stands to-day is likely to be preserved for historic associations. From December, 1921, to January, 1922 the members of Dáil Eireann debated in the examination room whether to accept or reject the Treaty offered by the Lloyd George Government and signed by the Dáil delegates. Much of the dispute went on in private : but the final session was open to the public and the Press, who had the extraordinary experience of watching a grave parliamentary decision taken when no one knew how the voting would turn.

That is perhaps the only historic association which University College, Dublin, can show to match Trinity College Dublin's long list. Yet nothing so important as that for Ireland ever happened within the walls of the older institution. And beyond doubt, at the present moment, the younger has the more important future—if the two are to continue for ever separate.

Even as it is a graduate of University College writes to me: " We have staffed the Revolution, the first Executive Council, the Supreme and High Courts, controlled the Imperial Conference and forced the Statute of Westminster (by Kevin

O'Higgins, McGilligan and Costello), carried through the Shannon Scheme, and provided the greatest prose writer of the day. Trinity, indeed!"

That is a strong case for the present importance of the predominantly Catholic institution, as against the predominantly Protestant.

For, although during the past century the doors of Dublin University have been open to all, without distinction of creed, Protestant Trinity is, and Protestant it is likely to remain : the University of a minority in Ireland. But there are, and I hope always will be, a good many of the majority who willingly accept the somewhat different way of life and of intellectual training that it offers. Some of these are influenced by the absence of a test which the National University imposes. Whoever matriculates there must pass an examination in Irish.

Undoubtedly when the National was established it was expected that it would provide the best equipped school for the study of Gaelic and of the Celtic languages and culture. Nationalist Ireland as a whole had been convinced by Douglas Hyde and his fellow-workers in the Gaelic League that it was a crime against nationality to let the Irish language die out—as it certainly was dying. Great voluntary efforts were made, and when the University was about to start on its work, a widespread agitation forced the governing Senate to make some knowledge of Gaelic obligatory for admission—with the obvious consequence that the subject must be taught in all schools.

There is so far this result. Irish is as generally known among educated Irish folk as French was fifty years ago. Irish history used to be written by men who knew no Irish, and were cut off from material of which even such a historian as Lecky scarcely knew the existence. Now the world at large begins to be aware that the Celtic culture, of which the Irish was the most important branch, has a great significance in world history. Students come from the United States to do valuable research work in Irish archaeology, and they do it with the assistance of the National University and the National Museum. A scholar trained in the National University has gone, since this book began to be written, to establish a school of Celtic studies in the University of Wisconsin. He was the son of John Dillon, who contributed more than any other man in Irish public life to create the University.

Work for the Irish language is by no means confined to the new University. Till a few months ago, Trinity College had for its Provost one of the most reputed authorities on the old language and literature. The best history of Ireland yet written comes from Professor Curtis of Trinity—a man fully equipped with knowledge of modern Irish. But the main central school of study is, as it should be, in the National University, with its colleges in Cork and above all in Galway nearer to the still living tongue—each college having its own fully equipped faculty of Irish.

About all this there is no disagreement. That begins when Ireland at large, and more particularly Dublin, considers the attempt which the Irish Government is making to force Irish back into general use by establishing it as the general medium for education. The underlying conception is that unless the Irish retain a distinctive language, Irish nationality will be obliterated and cease to exist. An army, it is said, must have its uniform. Yet we need not go far back to remember when Ireland was served by an army which had no uniform.

This is not the place to argue the matter fully; but two things should be said. Ireland exports fine horses and cattle, excellent whiskey and porter. But the fame of Ireland, Ireland's mark in the world, rests upon her export of men, not of beasts, of things spiritual more than of the spirituous. The best things she has are brain and muscle, and it is ill tampering with education. I do not admit that to be Irish it is necessary to have a knowledge of Irish, or even to have Gaelic blood. The idiom of the mind is more important than the idiom of the tongue—though one reacts on the other. No writer was ever more completely Irish than Shaw—not even that other Dubliner, James Stephens.

It is impossible to cut off a country from its

metropolis, and since Ireland had a metropolis in Dublin, the speech of Dublin has not been Gaelic. In the eighteenth century, when the greater part of Ireland was still Irish-speaking, Dublin was beyond yea or nay an English-speaking town. Certainly many people in it knew Irish ; Grattan's friend, Day, had to be taught by a foster-mother in Kerry and had to learn English when he went home. Lady Morgan's father, the actor Owenson, was one of the great attractions in the Dublin theatre for his songs in Irish, or in Irish and English mixed. But through all the centuries that Dublin has existed, it is doubtful whether Irish was ever the language most widely spoken there, and since it reached to a population of fifty thousand, there has been no question. I do not find that Dublin is any less Irish because English is and has been the speech of Dublin.

It would be comic if it were not disastrous to think of infants in Dublin being taught their rudiments in the " native language " which they never hear in their homes. Children so taught start life under a disability imposed on them by a theory which has no basis in real facts. Not so were educated the men who have been and are the leaders of modern Ireland. Mr. de Valera, Padraic Pearse, Douglas Hyde, got a natural education and with minds freely developed applied themselves to the study of a tongue which had a native attraction for them. The University has to consider that it must in the first instance supply Ireland with doctors, lawyers, civil servants and business men of supple, alert and well-nurtured intelligence ; and hitherto there has been no default. The groups of young men who in 1922 took charge of Ireland did, as a matter of historic fact, astonish these islands by their capacity. An Irish university has first-class material to handle, which deserves better than to have a servitude imposed upon it in the name of freedom. The obligation to teach and to be taught in Irish is nothing less than that in the city of Dublin, which at many moments and through many stresses has contrived to be rampantly Irish in the English tongue.

CHAPTER IX

THE CASTLE AND THE CATHEDRALS

DUBLIN CASTLE, as has been already indicated, stands for the oldest traditions in the city : it began as the fortress of the foreigner and it stayed so. "You may break, you may shatter, the vase if you will, but the scent of the roses will cling to it still." Ireland never liked the perfume of those roses ; and though the desire for ceremonial which is unduly starved in the Dublin of to-day may bring back St. Patrick's Hall into some decorative social uses, I cannot see Dublin Castle becoming again closely associated with the real life of Dublin.

Its two courts are full of offices, and secondary offices at that. But officials pullulate in all modern democracies. The Castle is approached from Cork Hill, which gets its name from Richard Boyle, Earl of Cork, the greatest of Elizabethan landsharks. He came to Ireland with twenty pounds in his pocket and saw his way to buying up grants of land that had been made to Walter Raleigh and other such adventurers ; and while they came to their various unlucky ends, Boyle prospered, and died an earl with four sons also in the peerage. But Dublin to-day has forgotten about him and would incline to give "Cork Hill" another derivation. One of Jimmy O'Dea's most popular witticisms described something as "like Dublin Castle—stone outside, cork inside." For all Dublin thinks that Cork men, with their deplorable quickness of intelligence, have got nearly a monopoly of civil service jobs.

However, there the Castle is, with its two courts, its two towers, the Record Tower and the Birmingham, the *ci-devant* Viceregal apartments on the south side, the *ci-devant* offices of the Chief Secretary and officers of the Household on the north. All these names belong to a vanished order of beings : but one may invoke some ghosts, without going back to the times when heads were exhibited conspicuously above the gateway.—They told Shane O'Neill in Elizabeth's day that his son's head was there. "My son has many heads," was the answer.

In the more peaceful days we meet the shade of Addison, who came over as Secretary. He and Swift had been friends in London, they spent pleasant hours together in Dublin and Swift hoped for preferment : but Addison was never a zealous friend. Later came Carteret, sent over as Lord Lieutenant by Sir Robert Walpole, anxious to be rid of a too brilliant colleague. He arrived when the famous Letter of " M. B. Drapier " had blown the agitation against " Wood's halfpence " to a flame of national protest, and Carteret had no

A RELIC OF MEDIEVAL DUBLIN—ST. AUDOEN'S GATE

ST. PATRICK'S MARKET (OLD STYLE)
By *Walter Osborne, R.H.A.*   Municipal Gallery.

choice but to offer high reward for discovery of the author and send the printer to jail. Swift stormed his way into the house and burst out : " Soh, my lord, what is this of your persecuting a poor printer ? " Carteret instantly quoted to him Dido's reply to Æneas : " *Res dura et regni novitas me talia cogunt moliri.*"—" Hard facts and the newness of my sovereignty constrain me to such courses." Swift, who worshipped wit, was disarmed. " What brings the like of you here ? " he said ; " get home and send us back our boobies."

Chesterfield of the Letters was at Dublin Castle, a Viceroy who left a good name. The rest are either insignificant, or men like Cornwallis, who stained a fine reputation by presiding unwillingly over the orgy of bribery at the Union.

But I come down to living memory and the period which was dominated by the figures of Gladstone and Parnell. Gladstone's first Chief Secretary after 1880 was W. E. Forster, who as a young man had done great work administering funds for the Society of Friends in the Irish famine. He came with friendly purpose, but inside of a year was known as " Buckshot Forster "—one of the many who lost a great reputation in Ireland. The man who made one there came five years later, under a Tory Government, Mr. Arthur Balfour, then regarded as a languid philosophical dilettante. Ireland found him iron painted to look like a lath : " Bloody Balfour." I was never at any time among the admirers of this admittedly great man, but in fairness I tell this story. Twenty years ago, in the Home Rule campaign before the War, a party of English Liberal politicians were touring round Ireland, and in Galway were received by the Chairman of the Urban Council— in all ways the biggest man in Connaught. I heard one of them ask him, " Which was the best of the Chief Secretaries you have known ? " " Arthur Balfour to be sure." The Liberal's face was a picture. " But aren't you a Home Ruler ? " " I am, of course," Martin McDonogh snorted back at him. " But he was the only one that ever did any good to Connemara."

The ablest agent that Mr. Balfour found was a Dublin lawyer, Edward Carson, who from being a prosecuting counsel soon rose to a law officer in Ireland, and in England a great advocate. Later, that Dublin man, whose instinct and audacity were superb, took the leadership of the Ulstermen and made their case for them to Great Britain as they could never have made it for themselves. Nobody who ever spoke to him could deny his charm ; the grim mask lit up delightfully. As to his ability, even his extremest opponents in Ireland have admired the boldness with which, when constitutional resistance failed him, he went on to the unconstitutional. But when his work had completed its consequences, Dublin Castle

for the first time was lost to the English rulers.
It is now little more than a museum piece, that
can be fetched out on occasion for historic curiosity ;
singularly ill-adapted to the conditions of a modern
administration.

Strangely enough the part in Irish history for
which Lord Carson will be always remembered
was not played in Dublin Castle, but against it—
when he led Ulster in revolt to upset the English
Liberal Government. In the last resort a Yorkshire lawyer, trained at Oxford and the English
Bar, was pitted against a Galway man, trained in
Dublin—and the Irishman won. A fortnight
before the European War broke out, conference
was held at Buckingham Palace between leaders of
the Government and leaders of the Opposition,
leaders of the Nationalists and leaders of the
Ulstermen, to reach a settlement on the Ulster
question. I met Redmond when he had come
from the first meeting : " Carson dominated the
whole," he said. " As an Irishman you couldn't
help being proud of him."

Another figure that one recalls then is that of
George Wyndham who, as Chief Secretary, decided that all the land of Ireland should pass to
the tenants by state-assisted purchase. This was
perhaps the only stage in the Irish revolution
accomplished through friendly agreement, and it
certainly helped that Wyndham was proud to be
a descendant of Lord Edward Fitzgerald and his

Pamela. He had indeed the traditional charm of the Geraldines, and as Rodin's bronze bust of him in the Municipal Gallery shows, a marked likeness to Lord Edward, though with a finer beauty. He was helped in the first measure by Sir Antony MacDonnell, an Irishman who had gained extraordinary reputation in the Indian Civil Service, and was established under Wyndham as permanent Under Secretary—head of the Castle administration. After Land Purchase, Wyndham planned with Sir Antony a half-way measure towards Home Rule : but his Unionist chiefs threw him over and he was one more man whom Ireland ruined. Sir Antony too—Lord MacDonnell (as he became)—got little but heartbreak for long attempts to be of service. A fierce imperious man, he said to Dillon that he had governed forty million Pathans ; it would be hard if he could not govern four million Irishmen. Dillon said that was not so certain.

After him came one of the most delightful Englishmen that ever lived, Augustine Birrell, who, like Wyndham, fell in love with Ireland. He carried the National University project—with the result that I have already suggested, of creating a hotbed of revolt. He was in charge during the War, and when the Easter rising took all the world by surprise, he had no choice but to resign ; and all the world blamed his slackness. Yet, twenty years after, when perhaps twenty men concerned in the rising have written their stories, there is one thing in which they all agree. So long as Birrell and his easy ways lasted, they could make no serious headway ; once he was dismissed, and the party of resolute government took control, the rebel movement spread like a house on fire.

There was a side to the life of Dublin Castle which Nationalists knew only by hearsay, but it is delightfully suggested in Lady Fingall's book of memories, *Seventy Years Young*. Very pleasant is the picture of young officers hunting out an old sedan chair to carry a pretty girl across the court-yard from the chambers where they dined to the great ballroom. All was a blaze of uniforms and silks and laces : and bright and early next morning, half the dancers would be off to follow the Ward staghounds, or hunt the Meath fox. The British army counted for a deal in all that gaiety and had its full share in the sport. Now the hunts go on without it, but not the elaborate ceremonial which cost most of the Viceroys from ten to sixty thousand a year over and above the allotted twenty.

Outside the Castle, the City Hall on Cork Hill belongs to a much later period—the mid-eighteenth century—designed by Cooley. It recalls chiefly the giant figure of O'Connell, who was elected as the first Catholic Lord Mayor, and who established a tradition that Catholics and Protestants should hold the mayoralty turn about. That compact lasted fifty years, but in the height of Parnell's movement a Protestant Lord Mayor refused to accept an address of congratulation to Parnell ; and thereafter the Nationalist city made sure that it should have a civic head in sympathy with its aspirations. Of other statues, one by Hogan, represents Thomas Drummond, one of the few Castle officials who is remembered with gratitude. Lucas, the patriotic writer who carried on Swift's work, has a statue by Edward Smyth, a Dublin sculptor. But I am concerned here with older monuments.

Dublin, which has two universities to meet its theological requirements, would naturally have two cathedrals. But it owns three, which does seem excessive—especially as two provide for the minority, perhaps one-fifth of Dublin's population.

I cannot feel that Christ Church belongs properly to the subject of this book, which is the life of Dublin. Historic landmark it certainly is, going back to the Dublin, half Danish, half Irish, of which Mr. Joseph O'Neill has written in his remarkable novel *Wind from the North*. In days when a Protestant Lord Mayor and a Protestant Corporation had their official pews there, it was officially connected with Dublin of the eighteenth century. But it belongs really to the period which opened with Strongbow and which ended when Dublin ceased to be a walled town. There are scores of curious things, as well as traces of fine medieval craftsmanship, to interest those who are concerned with the medieval city. To me the most interesting fact is that Christ Church was restored from ruins by whiskey; while St. Patrick's owed its reconstruction to porter. Mr. Henry Roe, the generous distiller who sent a cheque to Father Mathew, spent £200,000 on the restoration, which was carried out by Street—a specialist in Gothic. St. Patrick's was taken in hand by Sir Benjamin Guinness, head of the family which has done so well in Dublin and done so well for Dublin.

Another thing which has more than medieval significance is the reason why Christ Church needed rebuilding. The Normans built solid, here as everywhere else; but all the ground about the Liffey delta is a skin of soil overlaying a vast peat bog; and in the middle of Elizabeth's reign a cloudburst produced a bogslide and the south wall of the nave slid down towards the river. There is good reason to hope that we may never see sky-scrapers in Dublin.

Probably devout persons associated the building's collapse in 1562 with the fact that the English Liturgy had begun to be read there ten years earlier. In early Tudor days Christ Church must have ranked as Dublin's religious centre, for when Lambert Simnel came to Ireland and was accepted by the great Earl of Kildare as England's lawful king, they crowned the poor lad in Christ Church. And in the few months before the Boyne, when James II held court in Dublin Castle, Mass was said in Christ Church, but St. Patrick's was used to stable cavalry horses : Catholic Jacobites following the example that had been set by Cromwellian anti-clericals.

In all my recollection, St. Patrick's, the national cathedral, has counted for more in the city's life than the older church, which is the cathedral of the archdiocese. St. Patrick's has, for one thing, always prided itself on its choir, and musically-minded church-goers frequent there in spite of the fact that it is not easy to come at, standing away from the tram lines in a slum quarter, on low ground through which the river Poddle flows out of sight.

The great church has many monuments which a verger will exhibit, some going back to medieval times. But I suppose there is no other cathedral so dominated by the memory of one person : here Swift, being dead, yet speaketh. In one of the aisles is an inscription over the tomb of Schomberg, William III's general who fell at the Boyne, gallantly leading his men across : the epitaph tells in stinging Latin how the hero's relations would not, though asked again and again, pay for at least some memorial to so great a hero, but left this pious duty to the charity of strangers. Swift was accustomed to ask imperiously of great persons, and not accustomed to be refused ; he hated to put his hand in his own pocket, and this time he had to do it, with the rest of the Chapter.

There is also, now disused, the wooden pulpit

from which he preached ; and we know some of
the sermons which he preached from it. Here is
one. The preacher began thus :

In the ninth verse of the twentieth chapter of the
Acts of the Apostles it is written :

" And there sat in the window a certain young man
named Eutychus, being fallen into a deep sleep ;
and while Paul was long preaching he sunk down with
sleep and fell down from the third loft and was taken
up dead."

I have chosen these words with design, if possible,
to disturb some part in this audience of half an hour's
sleep, for the convenience and exercise whereof, this
place at this season of the day, is very much celebrated.

The accident which happened to the young man
in the text hath not been sufficient to discourage his
successors ; but because the preachers now in the
world, however they may exceed St. Paul in the art
of setting men to sleep, do extremely fall short of him
in the working of miracles, men are become so cautious
as to choose more safe and convenient stations and
postures for taking their repose, and trust rather
their destruction to a miracle than their safety. However, this not being the only way by which the luke-
warm Christians and scorners of this age discover
their neglect and contempt of preaching, I shall enter
expressly into consideration of this matter.

So the strong voice went on, loosing shafts of
reproof and satire :

A preacher cannot look round from the pulpit
without observing that some are in a perpetual whisper
and by their air and gesture give occasion to suspect
that they are in those very minutes defaming their
neighbours. Some lie at catch to ridicule whatever
they hear and with much wit and humour provide a

stock of laughter by furnishing themselves from the pulpit. But of all misbehaviour none is comparable to that of those who come here to sleep. Opium is not so soothing to many persons as an afternoon sermon. Perpetual custom hath so brought it about that the words of whatever preacher become only a sort of uniform sound at a distance, than which nothing is more effectual to lull the senses. For that it is the very sound of the sermon which hideth up their frailties is manifest, because they all awake so very regularly as soon as it ceaseth, and with much devotion receive the blessing.

Finally came the conclusion :

These considerations may perhaps have some effect while men are awake, but what arguments shall we use to the sleeper ? What methods shall we take to hold open his eyes ? Will he be moved by consider-ations of common civility ? We know that it is reckoned a point of very bad manners to sleep in private com-pany when perhaps the tedious impertinence of many talkers would render it at least as excusable as the dullest sermon. Do they think it a small thing to watch four hours at a play where all virtue and religion are openly reviled, and can they not watch one half hour to hear them defended ? Is this to deal like a judge (I mean like a good judge) to listen on one side of the cause and sleep on the other ?

Those who know Swift's record will have no doubt that when this last sentence with the em-phatic parenthesis was spoken, the fierce blue eye shot a glance from under the bushy eyebrows at some judge there present. For the law had been used often and unscrupulously to get the better of Jonathan Swift, and had failed.

The last word of the sermon condensed the last paragraph :

He that hath ears to hear, let him hear.

On the wall near the entrance door is the unforgettable epitaph which Swift wrote for himself in Latin ; beside it that which was written by another hand for Stella : and opposite to them are the actual graves of these famous and unlucky lovers.

Nothing preserves the sharpness of memory like a lasting question mark. We know that this stout middle-aged and rather deaf divine was loved devotedly by one charming and witty woman, and loved passionately by another. We are told that he was married to Esther Johnson, who in his Dublin circle was known as Stella ; but we have no actual proof of the fact. We know that they were life-long companions from the time when in Sir William Temple's household he taught this attractive small girl, probably a natural child of Temple's, how to write and to spell. We have the letters that he wrote her daily from London during a long absence and they are perhaps the best love letters in the world. But so far as can be ascertained, he and Stella never lived together as man and wife.

The other lady, " Vanessa," was Esther Vanhomrigh, whom he met in London. She fell violently in love with the famous wit, ran after him everywhere and finally followed him to

Ireland. Almost certainly she became his mistress. But the end after some years was a violent quarrel, followed shortly by Vanessa's death.

Novelist after novelist has tried to reconstruct the story, but in the end we have nothing beyond what is told in Vanessa's passionate pleadings and in Swift's poem " Cadenus and Vanessa," written for Vanessa's eye alone, but by her published. It gives the story of how that affair began and how it led up to her declaration. The poems to Stella, written for her birthday year after year, tell us only that this strange unhappy man loved her always and ran to her in all his torments.

His body was a torment, for throughout life he suffered from vertigo which brought on dizziness, roarings in the brain and fierce headache. Gradually worsening, it drove him in the end out of his senses—a fate that he always foresaw. His mind was a worse torment even than his body—a spirit made incapable of happiness by a passionate desire for power. Fame did not satisfy him. When his epitaph is read, it should be remembered that it was his custom always on his birthday to read the chapter of Job, which says :

> Let the day perish wherein I was born, and the night in which it was said, There is a manchild conceived.
> For now should I have lain still and been quiet, I should have slept.
> There the wicked cease from troubling, and there the weary be at rest.

An echo of that is in the epitaph's opening words :

" Here lies Jonathan Swift, dean of this cathedral, where savage resentment can no longer gnaw upon his heart." It is the cry of the satirist, all of whose self-expression has been in scourging humanity. But there is another note in the end of it. " Go, passer-by, and do if you can, like one who did his best for liberty."

Over against the east end of the cathedral, divided from it by a road and a blank wall, is the grim deanery house where most of *Gulliver* was written. Part of it was destroyed by fire, but not the small room on the first floor facing the cathedral, which was his study, nor the bedroom over it, where he sat writing down his thoughts the night after Stella died, till lanterns in the cathedral showed him that they were digging her grave, and he moved away from the sight of them to another apartment.

Beyond the cathedral is Marsh's Library, a charming room of the early eighteenth century, built by the Archbishop who ordained Swift. Swift read there often and there is a book annotated in his hand.

His memory is everywhere about this corner of Dublin and about the squalid streets, inhabited, now as they were then, by the very poor. But his chosen memorial is elsewhere. In his own words :

> He left the little wealth he had
> To build a house for fools and mad,
> And show'd by one satiric touch
> No nation wanted it so much.

DUBLIN OLD AND NEW

The sum which he bequeathed to found a hospital for the insane was only seven thousand pounds—wholly inadequate. But the Irish Parliament which he had lampooned individually and collectively in a savage poem called " The Legion Club " must have had Dublin's reverence for a great " characther " : they voted the money necessary to build St. Patrick's Hospital, beyond St. James's Gate on the road to Kilmainham. They built nobly in the best manner of the time ; and thanks to Swift, the unhappy humans to whom he in his last years belonged were sent to live in airy rooms, with spacious corridors to walk in, while London was still staring at lunatics thrown into railed pits on straw, like wild beasts. For more than fifty years Dublin was treating and curing mental disease in " Swift's Hospital " while nothing of the sort was attempted in England.

In the boardroom of that hospital the present director, Dr. Leeper, has gathered together portraits of Swift and of Stella and of Vanessa : with them is the desk taken from the deanery, at which *Gulliver's Travels* was written, and a charming inlaid box made for Swift by his friend Mrs. Delany, the authoress of famous memoirs, and on the outside is inset a portrait of Stella.

Any reasonable request for leave to view these treasures and others with them at the hospital will, I am sure, not be refused.

A very different order of ideas would need to

be handled if one discussed the high places of Catholic worship in this Catholic city. The Pro-Cathedral in Marlborough Street marks its provisional character by its title. Yet its opening was a triumph. Very few years after the passing of Emancipation this, the first great church built for the Catholics as a distinct denomination in Dublin, was opened. Daniel O'Connell, the Liberator, was, as he deserved to be, conspicuous in the ceremony. But the centre of it was the Catholic Archbishop Murray, to whom more than to any other man or woman—and men and women, lay as well as religious by profession, played great parts—was due the outward consolidation and organisation of a strong and living faith.

St. Patrick's and Christ Church stand there to-day charged with monuments and memories of famous and successful individuals. Marlborough Street, rightly looked at, has a deeper significance. It is a landmark in the story of the resurrection of a race.

CHAPTER X

DUBLIN'S PLEASURE GROUNDS

CERTAINLY Dublin does not lack open spaces. I have written already of the College Park, which is accessible to all by long standing permission. But Merrion Square and Fitzwilliam Square are rigorously kept for the surrounding householders. Fitzwilliam Square used to be open on payment when the Irish lawn tennis championships were played—a great social event in the last century when there was no country but Ireland to challenge English supremacy. So long as the Renshaw sovereignty lasted, no Irishman got beyond being runner-up at Wimbledon; the English players came over and won here in Fitzwilliam Square. But Willoughby Hamilton, still a figure on the Dublin Stock Exchange, won out at Fitzwilliam Square and then won even at Wimbledon. So a few years later did Joshua Pim, still practising as a doctor in Killiney.

Nowadays the tournament is held in the Fitzwilliam Club's own grounds and the Square no longer sees itself crowded for a week with Dublin's smartest dresses.

There is nothing exclusive about the most central and most famous of Dublin squares:

WEIR AND SALMON PASS AT ISLAND BRIDGE

THE LIFFEY FROM LUCAN HOUSE

ADMISSION PASSES TO SMOCK ALLEY THEATRE

LOCKET WITH ROBERT EMMET'S HAIR ENTWINED WITH SARAH CURRAN'S

DUBLIN'S PLEASURE GROUNDS

Stephen's Green has been the property of the Corporation since it was first enclosed.

Swift writes to Stella from London : " I wish dear M. D. would walk this morning in from Stephen's Green ; 'tis as good as our Park, but not so large." But later in the eighteenth century references to it are not all flattering. In 1779 a correspondent of the *Freeman's Journal* complains that the city has not one good place to walk in or one well paved street for driving. " If only Stephen's Green were enclosed by railings, like Lincoln's Inn Fields, instead of by a dangerous and noisome ditch, it would then become the ornament, instead of the grotesque, of this great city."

Snipe shooting there was forbidden as far back as 1760 ; but in 1814 it was " full of corncrakes." In 1851 it was said to be much improved, but still enclosed. In 1877 Sir Arthur Guinness, member for Dublin, got an Act passed which threw the Green open to the public. It was he who paid the cost of converting it into a charming landscape garden ; instead of dirty water which used to fill its ditches there is now a long narrow lake with a bridge across.

The statue of this benefactor (later known as Lord Ardilaun) adorns the Park. But the central group was an equestrian representation of George II, who never did Ireland either much harm or much good. This has lately been damaged by explosives,

12   161

but whether as a demonstration against the present King George or against Mr. de Valera is not clear.

The taste for demonstrating against monuments is strong, and for fear lest a new example of it should be given, the memorial to Kettle long stayed within doors. It was designed by the sculptor Albert Power, R.H.A., to stand opposite the Mangan memorial, of which Oliver Sheppard, R.H.A., is the artist, charmingly placed in a group of shrubs ; and now, happily, the design has been carried out. Observe the humorous upward glance from under Kettle's massive brow.

Stephen's Green is a place to stroll in or to sit about in and watch the ducks. But Dublin's far greater playground is outside the city, though the nearest corner of it, beyond Kingsbridge, just touches the Circular Road.

The Phoenix Park was originally part of the lands belonging to the Abbey of Kilmainham, and the lands were on both sides of the Liffey. After Ormonde's viceroyalty, the building lapsed into ruin ; some obliging person pointed out that the estate was a great expense of which he was willing to relieve the Crown and pay £10 a year. This was agreed ; later it was bought back from him— to his great advantage. The new purpose was to keep it as a deer park for the Lord Lieutenant, and accordingly it had to be walled in ; for economy, the Park was confined to the north side : land on the south bank was jobbed away to some other blood-sucker. Another parasite undertook to build the wall for £4,000, but charged £6,000, and then sent in a demand for £100 a year in perpetuity to keep it in repair.

The first residence built actually in the Park for the Viceroy's residence was where the magazine now stands—overlooking the Liffey, and it was called the Phoenix House. Dr. Chart disbelieves the current story that the place was really called Fionn Uisge (*Feen Uisk*), Clear Water, after a spring there, and that some scholar gave this fancy twist to the syllables. But Litton Falkiner, a good authority, accepts the Gaelic derivation.

The Phoenix House did not give lasting satisfaction and the Viceroys moved to Chapelizod, where Ormonde lived in state. That also was discarded and finally, about 1780, Government decided to buy the great Lodge which had been built by Mr. Clements, who had the post of Ranger. They paid him £10,000 for it—but this is no proof that he had built it at his own cost. Sir John Blaquiere, who came over as Chief Secretary with Lord Harcourt, stayed on after Harcourt's departure with a little job of fifty pounds a year to look after the letting out of grazing for cattle. He had, of course, several other jobs, paid in thousands, and no one knew why he wanted this small perquisite, till he set up a claim to a few acres on which to build a residence. On

these he built, at the public expense, the splendid
mansion which became the Chief Secretary's
Lodge. But when it was wanted for this purpose,
Blaquiere had secured so long a lease that they
had to pay him £7,500 to get possession. So the
Park developed, planned at first for the amusement
of the Irish Viceregal Court and exploited in every
direction for jobs and profiteering : but gradually
the public got its foot in.

In July, 1779, the *Freeman's Journal* wrote that
" under the rule of Mr. Clements every impro-
priety was rigorously expelled from that beautified
spot. Ill-looking strollers of either sex could never
get admittance at the gate except on public
occasions. Cars and noddies [the cheapest form
of shay] were refused passage. But now the
gates are opened wide to Tag, Rag and Bobtail.
The Sabbath is abused by permitting a hurling
match to be played there every Sunday evening,
which is productive of blasphemous speaking, riot,
drunkenness, broken heads and dislocated bones,
among ten thousand of the lower class ; and
meanwhile the deer are hunted by detached
parties of these vagrants and their dogs."

Elsewhere I find that the " Penny Boys " of
Smithfield proposed to have a bull baited in the
Fifteen Acres, and were laying bets that they would
draw a bigger crowd than the hurling match.
Mr. Eden, Lord Carlisle's Chief Secretary, com-
plains in 1782 that for some festive occasion " more

than two hundred whiskey tents " had been erected and had been allowed to remain, to the great detriment of the turf and of general amenity.

We manage these things better now. The Park is open for all sports and all classes. Polo, the rich man's game, is played there on a magnificent ground in front of the old Viceregal Lodge ; but the public are free to stand by the touchlines and watch one of the finest spectacles in the world. The Phoenix Park Cricket Club, Ireland's equivalent for the M.C.C., has its pavilion and its ground roped in and protected ; but the public can look on here also as they choose. Away out beyond this there are now football grounds past counting, some for the Association game, but mostly for Gaelic ; there are hurling grounds for men and women ; and when all this is said, whoever has a horse to ride can gallop to heart's content and find nothing in his way. Finally, there is the race-course : not many cities have one within two miles of the General Post Office. Like all else in the Phoenix Park, it gives the view of spreading green sward with timber scattered here and there, having for a background the northern end of the Dublin mountains, over which cloud shadows spread the peculiar charm of Irish landscape.

Lord Lieutenants and their company looked out at this fine prospect from the Viceregal Lodge through all the gay pre-war years that Lady

Fingall describes in her memories *Seventy Years Young*. To-day the Viceregal Lodge stands empty, something of a white elephant : it is a curious comment that the residence which Mr. Clements thought suitable for himself as Park Ranger now seems too big for the head of a State. Those huge rooms and the whole setting of the place really call for splendour, and splendour is not suitable to Irish resources. But dignity is well within our means, and the President that is to be will be housed in dignified surroundings at the old Chief Secretary's Lodge.

Sir Henry Campbell Bannerman was Chief Secretary at one stage of his career. In the last year of his life, when he was Prime Minister, he fell into talk at Westminster with the old Fenian, John O'Connor. "You know the Chief Secretary's Lodge, John O'Connor," he said. " I used to look out every day of my life across the park at the mountains and every day of my life I used to say to myself, ' What are you doing here ? ' " The old Liberal recognised that for all his good will he was an alien. But the elected President of an Irish State will see before him familiar beauty, a typical expression of the country which he represents, and will be there to give Ireland's welcome for Ireland to Ireland's guests. And it will be easier for Ireland's national head to settle in there because, after so many decades of official British occupation, the place has been through a moral disinfecting. It was occupied as the United States Legation by the representative of the one great Power which Ireland can never regard as foreign.

The Park has two special attractions of another kind. One is the charming little Zoo, not very rich in any way, except that it possesses well cared for and happy-looking beasts and birds. Irishmen who succeed well in the care of horses, hounds and cattle can manage also the great felines : and Dublin's Zoo has been greatly assisted in its finance by success, prolonged over generations, in breeding lion cubs. A lake adds to the pleasantness of the grounds.

At the main entrance nearest Kingsbridge, you will find on your right the People's Gardens, as well laid out with shrubs and flowers as Stephen's Green itself. But for the last word in Irish gardening you must go to Glasnevin, a lesser Kew, but not less flowery. Full advantage is taken of the soft Irish climate, kind to many delicate growths. The road to Glasnevin passes the famous cemetery where O'Connell, Parnell and many another Irish Nationalist leader lie interred. A reproduction of the historic Round Towers marks O'Connell's grave. Further along, before you reach the Horticultural Gardens, your road passes Delville, an old and historic house, though not a great one ; Swift was at the planning of it when his friend Dr. Delany decided to build here ; and Dean

Delany's wife wrote here many of the letters which, published long after, tell us much about the persons and manners of eighteenth-century Ireland.

There is another amenity of Dublin, which pertains to the city, though it is limited in ownership—the Royal Dublin Society's establishment at Ballsbridge. The grounds are used at different times in the year for different purposes : a dog show, a flower show, or in May the Spring Cattle Show, which draws almost the biggest attendances of all. The biggest are, of course, always for the Horse Show, at the beginning of August—Ireland's supreme celebration of the cult of the Horse. And indeed the Spring Show would probably not attract one-fourth of its attendance were it not that there were always jumping competitions as a side attraction in the big enclosure.

On these occasions all Ireland comes to Dublin ; the Border ceases to exist ; Ulster competes and very often wins both with cattle and horses. But all the world comes there in August. Ireland is one of the world's great cattle breeding countries ; it is the horse-breeding country *par excellence.* The proof of that can be had by anyone who goes to see the most superb event of all—the contests between teams chosen from the cavalries of different nations, competing for the challenge cup given by the Aga Khan. When I saw it last, nine teams were entered. The English, the German, the French, the Swedish and the Italians were, I think, all riding home-bred mounts. But the Canadians, the Swiss and the Belgians, as well as the Irish, were on Irish horses.

The enclosure is a great oval ; on two sides roofed stands run almost the entire length and are crowded, while by the rails all round people are massed three or four deep. On the west side, at the centre of the stand, is the President's box, and each team of four entering from the south-east corner rides half round the ring, and draws up at the salute before the representative of Ireland ; while the Irish Army Band, massed in front, plays the national anthem of the team. Applause welcomes the competitors before they ride back to the starting point and begin, rider by rider, the round of the ten obstacles.

I was in the Press stand opposite when the Swiss—who have often been winners—rode up and drew up gallantly ; the band started their national anthem, which is identical with the tune of " God Save the King." One of the horses, startled by the sudden burst of sound, plunged and tried to back away. There were roars of laughter all round me. " It's easy seen that's an Irish horse ! He doesn't like that tune."

Then came other teams and then, last but one, the English, and it was " God Save the King " again : but this time singing broke out from thousands of people, English and Irish, of the Unionist persuasion ; it was a kind of demonstration. When the Irish riders appeared and the Free State's national song was played, naturally enough there was a counter-demonstration, chiefly from the less fashionable side. But it lacked effectiveness, because the words of the " Soldiers' Song " are by no means so widely known as those of " God Save the King."

The final decision that day lay between the English and the Irish teams and my recollection is that it was won for the English by the horsemanship of a rider belonging to one of the best-known Anglo-Irish families ; and one may be very sure that all of those English-bred horses showed Irish blood in their pedigree not far back.

A period followed in which the English team did not compete because of unpleasantness arising from the " economic war." That " war " caused great inconvenience to all those concerned with horse-breeding on both sides of the Channel and on both sides of the Irish border : so great that the duty on the passage of horses through the Customs barrier has been done away with. Irish riders compete at Olympia with admired success and English teams are again welcome at Ballsbridge.

The fact appears to be that from a combination of soil and climate these islands can produce the best bloodstock ; and even countries like South America, where the horse introduced from Europe breeds and thrives like the zebra in Africa, cannot maintain the finest quality without constantly renewing the strain. And however it may be for cattle, certain districts of limestone country in Ireland are unequalled for horse-breeding—largely because the colts and fillies can live their early years completely in the open. Very little outlay is needed except the stud fee and the Irish Board of Agriculture sees to it that high-class stallions shall be available at moderate charges ; so that any day in the year hundreds of small farmers all over half of Ireland will have young horses running on wild pasture which one day may be made into hunters worth a hundred pounds. It is the poor man's gamble : but more than that, it is the glory of a poor man's possession.

I suppose many friendships are broken over horse-dealing : but surely every year friendships from all over Ireland are renewed at Ballsbridge ; for when you go there you are bound to meet folk from all parts of the country—and from any part of any country you ever knew. Dublin in August becomes a kind of Mecca, for those who have the cult of the horse and for those who have the taste for Ireland. With all modesty, we must admit that the taste is widespread.

CHAPTER XI

THE MUSEUMS

THE nineteenth century added to Dublin a remarkable apparatus of culture. First came, in 1864, the National Gallery, facing Merrion Square and touching Leinster Lawn. In 1890 were opened the fine buildings in Kildare Street which make two sides of the quadrangle in front of Leinster House. On the left, looking from the street, is the National Library, on the right the National Museum. But the great collection of Irish antiquities which is housed belongs to an institution founded in Grattan's day—or rather in Lord Charlemont's, for he was the first President of the Royal Irish Academy. The Academy's own premises and its library are in Dawson Street, but after a hundred years of existence the treasures that it had accumulated needed more space. It is by these that Dublin has unique interest for the instructed connoisseur.

A fourth institution, the Municipal Gallery, belongs to the twentieth century.

Of the four, the National Library is incomparably the most important to the life of Dublin. Trinity College up till fifty years ago reserved the privilege of reading in its library to its graduates :

even its own undergraduates were shut out. Conditions now are more hospitable there, but space sets a limit. There are too many books to allow of unlimited readers. The National Library is simply a well-furnished collection designed to be generally useful, but in the fifty years of its existence it has been directed with so much intelligence that a student will seldom fail to find what he wants there—especially on any subject relating to Ireland. There is also in formation there now a considerable collection of Irish correspondence.

But in the main the Library has been made to serve the student life of Dublin. T. W. Lyster, who was in charge here for some five-and-twenty years, had a missionary ardour for making books available ; and a remarkable group gathered about him. Dr. Praeger, his second in command, and then his successor, was botanist and geologist, but was (as his book *The Way that I Went* can show) curious about everything in Ireland, except perhaps, politics. Another member of the staff was the essayist, John Eglinton, now a member of the Irish Academy of Letters. He and the present librarian, Dr. Best, a Celtic scholar of note, figure largely in the sketches of Dublin life which George Moore and James Joyce have left on record. Anybody who reads Joyce's *Portrait of the Artist as a Young Man* will judge that the student population of Dublin buzzes about the National Library like bees before a hive ; anybody who goes to the place can verify this impression and can also find the most willing and intelligent help from all the staff and attendants that is to be found in any library. But except for those who are on pilgrimage to scenes mentioned in that modern classic *Ulysses*, there is nothing here to see. Across the courtyard it is a very different story.

The National Museum's Collection is highly miscellaneous and it contains many amusing things, like those seen in Paris at the Carnavalet—old costumes, coaches and the like. There are also objects of curiosity, like butter which had been dug out of some bog, preserved for centuries by the peat's action : there are for that matter human remains and antique plaid trousers on mummified legs. There are early types of boat, and similar survivals found by excavation about old lake dwellings. But it is useless to catalogue. The collection has two kinds of main interest. First, it contains the best-known specimens of Christian Ireland's decorative art as it had developed before the Norman Conquest brought in new ideas and new models, and also destroyed much of the old. Second, in addition to great accumulations of primitive work in stone and bronze, there can be seen here a collection of prehistoric gold ornaments richer than any in Europe except that at Athens.

Written records in Ireland begin with the coming of Christianity, fifteen hundred years ago. Beyond that, we have records elaborately compiled and transmitted by trained memory for several centuries at least before Christian scribes wrote them down. But we cannot say with any certainty how long it is since these brooches and torques were made and worn. All we know is that gold was plenty in Ireland, and that Ireland lay outside the track of the barbarian hordes who trampled down the Roman empire. Four hundred years later, when the Scandinavian pirates came, they found gold in Ireland to loot, and many examples of the Gaelic work have been discovered in Scandinavia.

Most of what is here to be seen, and I think all the primitive work, has been brought to light by chance. Things had been hidden when some raid was imminent : those who hid never had the chance to come back ; and there they stayed till spade or plough struck them. In 1854, when the railway from Limerick to Ennis was being built, a cache was opened in a cutting with hundreds of gold objects—few of which were preserved. The law of treasure trove did not then encourage finders to respect gold ornaments—the metal was melted and sold in a form that could not be traced.

Few of these objects come from tombs ; they had merely been stowed away. Dr. Praeger tells the story of one of the best finds. A boy and a dog started a rabbit in the limestone rocks of Burren, into which the rabbit fled ; the boy, peering in to see if he could get track of his chase, saw a yellow thing shining and brought home what his uncle declared to be brass work of an old coffin—unlucky to keep in the house : so it was pitched away. Two years later a District Justice, interested in antiquities, happened to pass and the matter was mentioned ; the boy remembered where he had thrown his find, hunted for it and produced " a gold gorget dating from about 700 B.C., of good size and quite perfect "—more than a foot across and weighing over half a pound ; but the work on it outvalued the metal. There it is now, in the National Museum.

So is a fibula or cloak fastener brought in from Balla in County Mayo. The schoolmaster was giving a class on the early history of Ireland, and showed a picture of one of these. A small boy said, " Please sir, I've got one. I found it in the bog." He had been using it as a toy.

But most famous is the case of the Broighter find. Where the river Roe flows into Lough Foyle there is flat land about its estuary and a man ploughing here turned up a cache of several objects—one being the model of a little boat with oars. He brought them to his employer, who gave him a few pounds for them, and then sold them to a known collector in Cork, who in his turn sold them to the British Museum. Now, if they were treasure trove, that is, a cache deliberately made to be recovered, they would belong to the Crown as representing the unknown next of kin : and the Crown had

NO RENT

BY ORDER of the EXECUTIVE,
Signed,

CHARLES S. PARNELL, President,
Kilmainham Gaol

A. J. KETTLE, Hon Secretary,
Kilmainham Gaol

MICHAEL DAVITT, Hon. Secretary,
Portland Prison

THOMAS BRENNAN, Hon. Secretary,
Kilmainham Gaol

JOHN DILLON, Head Organiser,
Kilmainham Gaol

THOMAS SEXTON, Head Organiser,
Kilmainham Gaol

PATRICK EGAN, Treasurer, Paris.

THE MANIFESTO ISSUED FROM KILMAINHAM GAOL IN 1881
Photograph of original poster.

PORTRAIT OF SWIFT BY AN UNKNOWN ARTIST
In Dr. Leeper's Collection at St. Patrick's Hospital.   Never previously reproduced.

made over its rights in Irish treasure to the
Academy. But if a man picks up what has been
casually dropped or thrown away, he is entitled
to keep it ; and when the Irish Academy tried to
recover them for the Museum, the British con-
tended that when the articles fell where they were
found, waters of Lough Foyle extended over that
place. Consequently—since it was not one object,
but a bunch of them—the inference was that they
had been thrown overboard as a votive offering.
Dr. Praeger was called in as a geologist to show that
the land where they were found stood as high
above water when these ornaments were made
as on the day when the plough unearthed them.
It was a great affair : Carson was on one side—
for Ireland ; Haldane on the other. I quote from
Dr. Praeger the Judge's finding :

> It is really extravagant to ask the Court to assume
> the existence of a votive offering of a sort hitherto
> unknown, in a land where such offerings are hitherto
> unknown ; in a sea not known to have existed for
> 2000 or possibly 4000 years, to a sea god by a chieftain
> both equally unknown, and to prefer this to the
> commonplace but natural inference that these articles
> were a hoard hidden for safety in a land disturbed
> by frequent raids, and forgotten by reason of the
> death or slavery of the depositor.

So the British Museum had to hand them over,
and Dublin can show you them.

The art which is preserved in these objects has
obvious kinship with the art of the pre-Christian

Irish epics. Indeed the epics describe precisely such ornaments. We can no more date accurately the poems than the ornaments : but, putting them together, we can know that skill in words, skill with the graving tool, and skill with the brush go back very far in the history of Ireland.

One thing to be noticed in the Museum is the great series of plaster casts taken from the sculptured crosses to be found in various parts of Ireland— some quite undamaged. The ornament on all is of the traditional Celtic type with entwined spirals ; but in some cases there are sculptured panels showing human figures. A French student, Mlle. Henry, has devoted a book to this aspect of Celtic art, showing that, as compared with other countries of Northern Europe—even with France—Ireland was in advance rather than behind the general level of artistic skill, between the eighth and tenth centuries. Wherever the crosses remain unmutilated, we recognise the fine sense of proportion and the decorative richness of the whole design.

From the tenth century to the twelfth Ireland's main business was to fight and to unite against the raiding barbarism of the Scandinavians who were destroying whatever they did not value enough to carry away. Later, after Brian's victory at Clontarf, the libraries began to be filled again, and among the most characteristic products of that age are the wrought and jewelled metal cases made to preserve either a treasured manuscript—

as can be seen in Trinity College—or some small
object of devotion : and so enshrined is the relic,
St. Patrick's Bell.

It is known that the saint, on his journeying
through Ireland, carried with him a bell for ritual
use ; and this bell, simple and unpolished as the
saint's own Latin tongue, was preserved at Armagh
as the very one used by him. The shrine for
it was made in 1091, some eighty years after the
battle of Clontarf, with all the skill that Ireland
could then show.

But in 1932, when the fifteenth hundredth anni-
versary of Patrick's coming was to be celebrated,
the Catholic world held its Eucharistic Congress
in Dublin. Mass was said by the Pope's Legate
in the Phoenix Park, before a kneeling audience
of some quarter of a million people ; but the
words of the Mass, sung or spoken, were relayed by
wireless to every back street in Dublin, to every
little village from Donegal to Kerry. For that
occasion St. Patrick's bell was brought out of its
shrine and struck at the high moments of the Mass ;
the sound of it reached all over the island—further,
it may be, than even Patrick ever set his travelling
foot.

I do not dwell on the variety of ornaments in
the Museum, of Christian or pre-Christian times ;
there are always skilled attendants to direct a
visitor ; but to illustrate the historic development
of Celtic art, look at the Cross of Cong, made in

County Roscommon by a monk whose name is inscribed on it, to hold a fragment of the true Cross. The date can be fixed to about fifty years before the Norman Conquest; and the reliquary was preserved in the Abbey of Cong on Lough Corrib, where Rory O'Connor, the last High King of Ireland, who made submission to Henry II, ended his days.

Here, as with the " Book of Kells," a magnifying glass is needed to realise the fineness and intricacy of the involved spirals. It represents the culmination of Gaelic art and craftsmanship, so far as we have means of judging; for destruction was wholesale. Cong escaped, outlying and hard to reach, guarded by lake and by mountain in a district where Irish is still the normal speech. The abbey was suppressed like the rest, but like others in Connaught was tolerated even down to the time of the penal laws; and in the nineteenth century the old parish priest was titular abbot of Cong. In his custody the priceless jewel remained : it was brought at Mass times into the parish chapel. Sir William Wilde, whose taste for Gaelic antiquities showed itself when he called his son Oscar, had a house on the shore of Lough Corrib, near Cong, and he of course knew of the relic, stored in the old priest's cupboard. He it was who persuaded the old man to part with it for a sum to be spent on necessary chapel repairs, and the cross went off with him to the Royal Irish Academy, where it was housed with honour in a glass case.

But the people of the parish were resentful, and thought that luck would leave them ; and a tall young curate, wild as a mountain bull, was angrier than they. He took the train to Dublin, visited the Academy and stayed long scrutinising the relic in its case : there was a smash of glass and the tall young man in the big frieze coat was seen hastily leaving. The cross had to be retrieved. The parish was promised and received a careful copy of it in water colour. No doubt all is for the best ; but my heart goes out to the curate. Sir William Wilde was a remarkable man and a great Dubliner ; but in his day, when there was occasion to relay the flooring of St. Patrick's, he and other antiquarians profited by the chance to open Swift's coffin and make a medical examination of the skull ; they took out Stella's too while they were about it, and conversaziones were held at which these interesting relics were shown and handed round.

After the Normans came, the peculiar Gaelic ornamentation tended to disappear ; new artistic forms came in with the pointed arch. But in literature, the same instinct led Irish poets into more and more formidably complicated patterns of rhyme and alliteration ; and when these same Irish poets wrote in English on occasion—Owen Roe O'Sullivan for example—they attempted in English to do the same thing—contrary to all the genius of the language. They were only half-educated men—though they might know Latin, or even Hebrew. But it seems to me that in a writer of our day, whose culture is far-reaching and whose mastery of the English tongue is astonishing, we find the same characteristics breaking out. Yet the artist who evolved all those intricacies of line and colour in the " Book of Kells," and the other who twisted threads of wire into delicate patterns to hold jewels or enamel in the Cross of Cong, were artists happy in the utter concentration on their task ; but the mind which jumbled words and thoughts into such bizarre and profuse medley for the story called *Ulysses* seems to me to be orchestrating Bedlam. Yet in the tireless inexhaustible mastery of his involved craftsmanship, Joyce seems to be a true descendant of those old monks.

Dublin craftsmanship of modern times ranked high when it had rich patrons. The delicate sensitive plaster mouldings of the eighteenth century were done by Dublin workmen. Horace Walpole sent his books over to be bound by skilled Irish hands. In the metal craft, Irish-wrought silver was beautiful and the Museum has examples ; or without going to a collection, West's shop in Grafton Street has always many reproductions of the old models—and a knowledge of the subject long transmitted ; for this firm has existed since the eighteenth century.

Irish Lace can be seen also at the Museum.

In the art of painting, which is comparatively

modern, Ireland has not been distinguished, and whatever Dublin has to show in this kind of native work was done in living memory. It is true that Maclise and Barry and Sir Martin Shee were all Academicians and all Irishmen ; but that does not give Ireland anything to set against Raeburn. Ireland was far off from access to the classic masterpieces and in 1864 steps were taken to give more facilities for those who wished to study : the National Gallery was built and endowed. Gradually a collection has been amassed which, thanks to the discernment of such directors as Walter Armstrong and more specially Hugh Lane, can hold its own with what is to be seen in the secondary European capitals—in Budapest for instance. Many and many a Dubliner has made first acquaintance here with the great Italians, Spaniards, Flemings and Dutch : George Bernard Shaw has written of spending long hours in the National Gallery " when I was a dreaming boy." There is perhaps nothing of the first importance— though I do not know many pictures more easily remembered than Goya's rakish lady in her black veil.

One work of quite modern times has an incidental celebrity. During the European War, Sargent offered as his contribution to some war fund a blank canvas on which he would paint any portrait specified for ten thousand pounds. Hugh Lane was in the United States and persuaded President

Wilson, then the most conspicuous of living men, to be the sitter. It is in no way one of Sargent's best works and suggests Wilson's underlying weakness rather than his missionary power : yet it was a fine gift from Lane to his country and to the Gallery of which he had been director.

Attached to the National Gallery is the National Portrait Collection, of which, since I am writing of Dubliners, it is more reasonable to write fully. Here are the portraits of many who played a great part in Dublin's life—sometimes of high value as pictures, sometimes merely of interest as a likeness. Curran's head is here, suggesting well enough what Charlotte Brontë called him—" the ugliest man that could be imagined and perfectly irresistible." Here is Parnell, painted by Sydney Hall from a series of sketches made while Hall was working for the *Illustrated London News* during one of the endless trials. Here also the artist, Miss Purser, R.H.A.—perhaps the most brilliant of a Dublin family, distinguished in many lines—shows us Roger Casement, though perhaps not even she has done full justice to the beauty and distinction of that knight errant who passed through such vicissitudes of praise and execration before he died for Ireland on the gallows. Here is Kuno Meyer, the Gaelic scholar, who worked for long in Dublin at the revival of Irish learning, and who during the war joined with Casement in an attempt to make captured Irish soldiers join the German

side. They addressed the men, to whom naturally
strong inducements were offered by the Germans ;
they appealed to Irish sentiment and then Meyer
said : " Is there anyone here who can sing an Irish
song ? " A sergeant stood out and said he could :
so Meyer brought him on the platform. But what
he sang was " God Save the King " and the
whole muster joined in. Meyer, I think, Casement,
I am sure, were generous enough to admire
that answer, and give it its true meaning.

The portrait of Meyer is by Augustus John, and
if there is a better portrait by him, I have not seen
it. The man's geniality and sensitive appreciation
of beauty are there as well as the massive intellect.
Near it is a portrait of Walter Osborne by himself—
almost the only sitter whom he tackled freely ; for
this delightful artist was essentially a painter of
fields and of animals in them, and of the atmosphere
in which all were bathed.

Sooner or later this collection will be greatly
reinforced by other portraits which are at present
in the Municipal Gallery at Charlemont House.
The story of this Gallery has been told often, but
has to be kept on record.

About 1904 a letter from Hugh Lane appeared
in the Irish press, pointing out that a great collection of modern French painting was about to be
sold. Dublin had its National Gallery, with no
work in it later than that of Reynolds. No student
of literature would be content if his access to

books stopped at the age of Samuel Johnson. Lane proposed that a fund should be raised to acquire the whole collection as the nucleus of a gallery of Modern Art : and that the Corporation should undertake the upkeep of it.

The proposal was warmly backed by Yeats and Lady Gregory. Dublin at large knew nothing of Lane except that he dealt in pictures. We were perplexed by the fact that an unknown young man was proposing as his contribution to present pictures whose value admittedly ran into thousands. But it was settled that the collection should be brought over and displayed in the Royal Hibernian Academy's Gallery (since burnt down) and there was no possible mistake about the quality. Nearly all were French, ranging from Corot and others of the Barbizon School—Diaz and Rousseau—to the impressionists, Monet, Sisley, Renoir, Manet and the rest. A good many were bought, Lane gave others, and others again he proposed to leave in the Gallery on loan. The Corporation agreed to strike a rate for upkeep, but no permanent building was available. A house in Harcourt Street was taken as a temporary measure, but Lane insisted that a special gallery should be built, as a condition of his completing the collection.

There were delays. The circle about Yeats and Lady Gregory knew, all artists knew, that Lane was a young man with unerring instinct for beauty and also a technical power of recognition which enabled him often to buy for ten pounds what was worth a thousand : they knew that money acquired in this way he spent in buying and buying works new as well as old, always with infallible judgment ; and that, living like an ascetic, he gave away as fast as he bought. One may put it that the purpose of his life was to diffuse beauty and make it accessible. Nowadays, he is dead and we all know this, but at the time it was not easily believed ; and an ugly ignorant press attack on him, hindered at first all schemes for the Gallery. Fresh controversy arose over a proposal to build it on a bridge over the Liffey ; and finally Lane emigrated in anger to London, taking with him the best pictures and leaving sad gaps in the Harcourt Street collection, which he had made into a complete representation of fifty most important years in the history of modern painting. But his friends in Dublin always hoped to get Lane back—and also the pictures, which meantime had been lent to the Tate Gallery.

Then came the War : Lane went to America, and returning in the *Lusitania* was drowned. His will was found, leaving the thirty-nine loaned pictures to the National Gallery in London—of which the Tate is a branch. But a codicil had been added, apparently before he sailed, revoking this clause and leaving them to the Dublin Municipal Gallery. The codicil was signed and not witnessed ; it is therefore legally invalid. The trustees of the British Museum had no choice but to stand on their strict legal right.

There was however fierce agitation. Lane had heaped benefits on galleries in England and in the Dominions ; it seemed ugly to disregard his last wish. The Government set up a parliamentary Committee to enquire if the codicil really represented Lane's fixed intention. The Committee found that it did represent his intention. But they reported also that in their judgment he would have changed it had he lived. One must say in fairness that this was written after the Custom House and Four Courts and the Hibernian Academy had been destroyed.

Government did not think proper to propose the Bill which would be necessary to give the codicil legal effect, and now several of the disputed pictures are in prominent places, not only in the Tate, but in the National Gallery itself.

Meantime Lane's conditions as to the provision of a special gallery remained unfulfilled. But under Mr. Cosgrave's government the Custom House was rebuilt ; it was decided to transfer there the paper machinery of the Census which had long been lodged in Charlemont House. This left Charlemont House vacant, and Miss Purser, on learning this, made one swift swoop. Mr. Cosgrave agreed that if the Corporation would like to have the building for a Municipal Gallery, they should get it ; leaving to them the cost of reconstruction.

The result is the present Municipal Gallery, occupying the whole of what was Charlemont House and also the quadrangular courtyard with its front and wings enclosed : and there now is Dublin's collection of modern pictures and statuary —notable even in its mutilated condition. A good deal has been added since it was first housed in Harcourt Street ; for Lane not only gave, but persuaded his friends to give—Steer, for instance, who is superbly represented. But my concern is with the work of modern Irish artists who are either still living or were alive when the collection was formed.

The most interesting case is that of Nathaniel Hone. In the National Portrait Gallery there is an admirable self-portrait by Nathaniel Hone of the eighteenth century ; he painted Horace Walpole amongst others. In the mid-nineteenth century, another Nathaniel Hone went to Paris to study art and lived and worked with the Barbizon group ; he had the lease of Corot's studio during the Franco-Prussian War. Then he came back to Ireland, a man of means, with a handsome place near Malahide, and he continued to paint and to exhibit, but, being wholly without ambition, exhibited only in Dublin. In the Hibernian Academy his pictures, mostly of squally seas, and rain storms roughly indicated, puzzled most of us by their total unlikeness to anything that was shown with them. I know now that Hone painted a shower much as Monet, another heavy-handed artist, would have done—but with the same force and intense observation.

When the Staats Forbes collection was brought over, Lane showed among the French pictures a couple of canvases by the Irishman who had worked with them ; we knew then where he belonged, and saw that he held his own there. One of these pictures is now in the Municipal Gallery, a heavy dark-winged sunset over the sea about Malahide. But there are of course a dozen of his scattered among the work of younger Irish artists, which harmonise ill with them. I should like to see him hung with the French impressionists—a painter of their school and of their calibre, and one whose work is probably in no gallery outside of Dublin.

Here again I must not catalogue : but there is beautiful work here by Walter Osborne ; there are portraits, and better still the study of a Dublin street arab, by John Butler Yeats, the poet's father ; pictures by Jack Yeats, the poet's brother ; pictures by Paul Henry, pictures by Grace Henry, pictures by Keating—all among those living who count. Also of course there are pictures by William Orpen, the most successful artist that ever came out of Ireland and I think the best. He was born and bred in Dublin, trained in Dublin up to a point ; I have seen early work of his as like an Osborne as he could make it ; but then came

Paris and London. There is nothing here I think characteristic of him at his best ; that is to be found in his series of war pictures, things as good as any of Daumier's. But there is a whole series of portraits here by him of the men prominent in Dublin at the beginning of the century, Mahaffy for instance. Some day some of them will go to the Portrait Gallery. With them will go much that now fills the long room which was kept empty for years to house the " Lane pictures " when they are restored—as I think they will be in some day of reconciliation.

For the present, Sir John Lavery's great gift is here—a gift in memory of his beautiful and witty wife : a witty woman who never said an unkind thing and who was devoted to the cause of Ireland. In one of the outer rooms there is a picture of her by Lavery in the flower of her age, working outdoors, palette in hand—for she also was a painter, and in the big room is an excellent portrait by her of her husband. The other studies in that room are Lavery's representations of the men, English as well as Irish, who had most to do with the Treaty of 1921 and the foundation of the Free State. Perhaps the best of them is a portrait of Mr. Healy. But I should not be sorry to see them transferred to the other gallery—and overjoyed if it was to make room for the Lane bequest. Only one thing should stay always in Dublin's gallery of modern art—the painter's study of his wife as she lay on her deathbed. Incapable of remaining anywhere for a length of time without painting, incapable of staying away from her bedside, he did what was as natural to him as breathing and put his feeling on to the canvas. The result is of heart-rending poignancy and beauty.

I have spoken elsewhere of Epstein's bust of Lady Gregory and Rodin's head of Wyndham (there are five Rodins in this little gallery). No one should fail to notice a head in terracotta by Hughes of the poet " Æ " at nineteen. Nor, for that matter, John Yeats's early study of the lank youth with disorderly tie, his son, the poet.

A young English artist whom I brought there lately was most impressed by the great Mancini portraits of Hugh Lane and his sister which face each other across the long transverse gallery. But indeed the place is Hugh Lane's monument— incomplete until his last wish is carried out. It is a fine thing for any gallery to own Manet's " Eva Gonzales " or Renoir's " Les Parapluies," or Daumier's " Don Quixote," and now Trafalgar Square has them. But it is not a fine thing to hold them by a legal quibble against the admitted will of a man to whose deliberate bounty the Gallery where they hang is heavily indebted for undisputed gifts.

For those who desire to study the work being done by living artists, there is the annual exhibition

THE OLD CHIEF SECRETARY'S LODGE

THE FRONT OF LUCAN HOUSE

DRAWING-ROOM AT LUCAN HOUSE

ROUND ROOM AT LUCAN HOUSE

held by the Royal Hibernian Academy each spring in the School of Art, next door to the National Library : its own building unhappily perished with many valuable works of art in the flames of Easter 1916. There are also pictures constantly to be seen at Mills' Gallery in Merrion Row ; at the Dublin Painters' room in No. 7 Stephen's Green ; at a gallery attached to Messrs. Combridge's good bookshop in Grafton Street ; and in the hall and lounge of the Shelbourne Hotel.

But I note also two centres of a special art for which within this century Dublin has become distinguished—the designing and manufacture of stained glass. Messrs. Clarke's studio in North Frederick Street was old-established ; it became illustrious by the talent of the late Mr. Harry Clarke, who died unhappily in the full strength of his age, but not before his gift for design and amazing instinct for securing depth and brilliancy of colour had been shown in many completed works. The finest example known to me in Dublin is in St. Joseph's Church, Terenure, opposite the terminus of the main Rathmines tramway ; but anyone who passes on from Dublin to the Atlantic coast will find one even more remarkable in the great church of red sandstone at Newport on the Mayo coast. That building and the window combine to take away the reproach of artistic insignificance from modern church building in Ireland.

The other studio, An Túr Gloine (that is, the Tower of Glass) in Pembroke Street, depends less on the excellence of a single talent. Under the directing impulse of the portrait painter, Miss Sarah Purser, a group of art workers was formed to work co-operatively ; and for some thirty years they have been sending this glass and mosaic to churches, Protestant and Catholic, in all parts of Ireland, and to places so far as Canada—even to Singapore. A common character has, I think, been set on the work, perhaps the mutual influence of the group, perhaps by the supervision of the long experienced artist who was its founder ; but each window is in all its parts designed and executed by one craftsman — or craftswoman. Opinions vary whether the best work of An Túr Gloine has been done by Mr. Michael Healy or by Miss Geddes— or, again, by some other of this gifted group. But beyond doubt the concerted movement to make church builders seek their ornament in Ireland instead of importing it from the Continent was originated and inspired by the artist who brought the group together in An Túr Gloine and kept them together.

No reproduction in black and white can give any real idea of an art whose essence lies in colour ; but photographs will be found here of a window by Miss Geddes in St. Anne's Church, Dawson Street, and of one which was designed by Harry Clarke for the Hall of Doctors at Geneva. Clarke's purpose was to illustrate the writings of modern Irish writers from Shaw and Yeats to Joyce and O'Flaherty; but the Irish Government thought this treatment of Irish types too bizarre; so this beautiful piece of iridescent colour and intricate design remains where it was executed, at the studio in North Frederick Street.

Another craft to which artistic talent has been happily applied in Dublin is the making of hand-knotted woollen carpets—first introduced into Ireland by a true benefactor, the late Mr. James Morton of Darvel. The Donegal carpets were widely known before Miss Gleeson decided to take up the industry in Dublin and bring into the designing of these costly fabrics inspiration from the old Celtic ornaments. The new Irish State has given full patronage to her labour and that of her fellow-workers at Dun Emer in Hardwicke Street; for Dun Emer carpets may be seen in London on the floors of the High Commissioner's office, and in Dublin, even more impressively, they carpet the Dáil with rich colouring and deep mats of wool soft to the tread.

Allied in inspiration are the Cuala industries in Lower Baggot Street where the Misses Yeats, sisters of the poet and painter, produce hand-printing and coloured cards of great beauty. Many works by W. B. Yeats have been issued in this costly and dignified form.

All these are perhaps examples of art rather than

craft. But there survives in Dublin one craft directed with a fine artistic feeling—the making of poplins. Dublin of the eighteenth century was full of weavers ; in the old quarter about St. Patrick's one may still see houses in very poor streets with the tall windows on the first floor, planned for the worker at his loom. Mass production has swept them all away : only this small industry survives, making exquisite and durable fabrics in two or three small establishments, of which the most important is owned by Messrs. Atkinson, and its products can be seen at their shop next door to the Ulster Bank in College Green.

CHAPTER XII

DUBLIN BAY AND THE LIFFEY

Two things have made the fortune of Dublin—its bay and its river.

I need not dwell on the beauty of the bay : that is a delight to anyone who approaches our capital by the mail-boat service, with moderate luck as to weather. But it should be realised what Dún Laoghaire is, and is not. It is a landing place which can be approached at high speed by vessels of a certain draught—and the Irish mail-boats, drawing more water than any of the cross-channel services to France, are by so much the steadier. It is also a great yachting harbour and anchorage. But it is not the port of Dublin.

I cannot regret that most visitors to Ireland get their first impression this way—such is the beauty of that background, from Howth to Killiney. Yet it is an interesting experience to come by water into the heart of a great town, and those who sail to Dublin from Liverpool or Glasgow (excellent services) will find this entry very pleasant of a fine morning : and neither Liverpool nor Glasgow have any building by their quays comparable to the Custom House which Gandon built for John Beresford. Yet both Liverpool and

Glasgow have the advantage of Dublin in that they are built on ground which rises steeply. Dublin lies too low to be well seen from the water ; and of course there is no comparison possible between the Liffey's estuary and either the Mersey or the Clyde.

What should be pointed out, however, is that Dublin has made the best of a difficult position with skill and resolution. Ireland is richly provided with natural harbours, but Leinster is not. North, South and West in Ireland, the Atlantic brings deep water to a rockbound coast, having in it cliff-sided openings. But on the east there is shoal water everywhere for miles out, and between Carlingford Bay on the edge of Ulster and the Waterford river which divides Leinster from Munster, you will scarcely find anything to be called a cliff. The land slips down league after league to blend gently with the shore.

What exceptions there are will be found in Dublin or near it. From the long range of mountains lying north to south, three rocky spurs run eastwards ; one ends in Wicklow Head, another, twelve miles south of Dublin, continues the line of the Sugar Loaf peaks to the serrated ridge of Bray Head—making the central feature of Wicklow's beauty. But neither at Wicklow nor Bray is there a good harbour, even for fishing boats. It was the northernmost of these spurs, coming down to the beautiful hill of Killiney and so to the rocky shore from Dalkey to Dún Laoghaire, which created a possible landing place for considerable craft in the south corner of Dublin Bay. This same rock formation continues under water ; it thrusts up a crest in Dalkey Island, and then, six miles away, appears again, emerging in the mountain peninsula of Howth, which has cliffs in good earnest to face the sea.

Howth, projecting far eastward into the Channel, makes a shelter from the north ; but its little harbour is on the north side, sheltered by one more rocky outcrop, Ireland's Eye. Here the fishing fleet works : and here, before steamboats began, the mail packets from Holyhead, or from Parkgate, near Chester, often landed their passengers. The way to Dublin's own quays was made difficult and dangerous by a bar of silt and sand, accumulated where the Liffey discharged into the shallow bay ; and vessels, lying off to wait for favourable wind and tide, were often caught by bad weather from the south and driven on to the long ridge of sandhills by Clontarf, which has been called the Bull from time immemorial : Clontarf means the " Bull's Strand."

As early as Grattan's day, Dublin's enterprise had carried the South Wall down for two miles, so as to deepen the channel ; and if the weather served, Viceroys made their state landing there. When Beresford built the new Custom House, extension of the North Wall was part of the scheme ;

and through six or seven generations since then the North Wall has been extending ; other moles run out from it to bank the water in and dredgers have been constantly at work. In our time, Sir John Purser Griffith, chief engineer to the Port and Docks Board, and known as one of the great men in the engineering profession, for uncounted years was constantly at work. Thanks to him, and thanks to the Board for which he worked, it is now possible on occasion for a fifteen-thousand ton liner to take passengers on board by gang plank in a river that had not safe anchorage for craft of three hundred tons when the Custom House was building.

It is a pleasure to note also that Dublin is developing the amenities of its bay. If you land at Dún Laoghaire and go by car or by motor bus to your hotel, the first three miles will take you along the water's edge by a well-made avenue, free from heavy traffic. Beyond that, at Blackrock, you must join the main tramline : but one may hope that since these suburbs are now included in the city at large, the roadway by the water will be continued so as to join the fine stretch of Merrion Avenue and lead this traffic up to the Dodder at Ballsbridge.

On the north side, the way out leads necessarily through a quarter about Amiens Street Station which is all reclaimed slob and can never be beautified. The strand along which Swift used to ride when he went to visit his friends, the Grattans, at Belcamp (uncles of the patriot) came pretty nearly up to where the tramline now runs. A great building rising out of slums to your left as you go towards Clontarf is Aldborough House— one of the greatest city mansions, built in the Grattan period by a very eccentric nobleman. It marks the furthest limit to which fashionable building was then pushed along this slope of ground—and it surely was pushed beyond discretion. Nowadays this once splendid palace houses an engineering section of the General Post Office.

Beyond this, the tramline, running over the ground where the battle of Clontarf was fought, brings you to the little Tolka river. After the battle, Brian's grandson was found in the bed of it, still in death-grips with a Dane ; each had tried to drown the other and each succeeded.

From here a space to which the tide had access under the railway embankment used to be a horrible swamp ; now, filled in by the city's refuse, sown and planted over, it is a very passable park and playground for the children of a suburb rapidly growing here. In the same way, beyond the railway embankment, a belt along the shore to Dollymount is being fenced in to make a pleasant promenade. Ultimately too, no doubt, a drive will be carried along where only the tramtrack now runs, linking up Dollymount to Sutton, on the sandy neck which joins Howth to the flat land.

I shall not write again about Dublin Bay. But anyone who has only a short time in Dublin and wishes to see one of Ireland's most famous beauty spots can take a tram or bus to Howth, and be carried by the tram to the summit, some five hundred feet up, on that mass of rock and gorse and heather. From here he has a view north and north-west over Ireland's great central plain ; on a clear day he will see, fifty miles off, the blue silhouetted line of the Mourne mountains. South-ward and south-west, from the cliff top, he looks across half a dozen miles of blue water to the smoky mass of Dublin, with spires rising from it ; to the brown and purple huddle of the Dublin mountains, and beyond Dún Laoghaire, to the marvellous serrated line which the Sugar Loaf peaks continue from Bray Head up to where it merges in the general mountain mass.

Or if you prefer to look at it the other way, a bus will take you almost to the top of Killiney Hill ; climb to the top, and look south over the wide Vale of Shanganagh below you, with Bray Head and Sugar Loaf bounding it on the farther side, while westward, where its little river rises, it narrows into the deeply wooded Dargle and the intricate beauty of Powerscourt demesne. Then, when you are tired of that, look north and north-east across blue flashing water to the fine craggy slope of Howth, whose outer limit is a lighthouse perched where once was a stronghold of the Gael : Dun-

criffan means the Fort of Crimthann, one of the
pre-Christian kings who raided the Roman empire's
ports in Britain and in France, till in one of these
raids they made capture of the slave Patrick, who
was to subdue his captors and alter the whole
current of Ireland's life.

I leave the bay now to talk about the river—
which is by no means so invariably praised. To
be plain, the Liffey used to stink to high heaven ;
and literature is full of allusions to this fact. Well,
it does not stink now. Whether the Port and
Docks Board is to be thanked or the Dublin
Corporation, I know not ; but a good job it was.
I am not saying that the exhalations of a tidal
river cramped between quay walls in a big town
are like the breath of that same river when it flows
between grassy banks or among slopes of heather
(and the Liffey does both), or like the sea's breath,
into which it will soon be merged. But the Liffey
is no longer offensive, and when sunset reflections
are caught in it under the dome of the Four Courts,
of an afternoon, it can be decorative. Still, to
look at it, no one would say it was a salmon river,
but it is one ; it was a better salmon river in the
days when every salmon must have been in a
hurry to get away from the necessity to hold its
nose. But people still can and do poach salmon
with nets in front of the Four Courts ; they poach
them in front of Guinness's Brewery, where all
the little barge craft with broad red bands on their

funnels make such a handsome and a cordial show. Also above Kingsbridge, people net them legitimately : holders of a very old right to fish what is called the Salmon Pool.

Here, about a mile upstream from the railway terminus, the river is held up by a long dam, set at an angle to its course, with sluice gates ; for the Liffey comes down off a great mountain catchment area and can be terrible and sudden in flood. Near the end of the dam, on the north bank, the sill of the weir is cut down by a matter of six inches for a breadth of some five feet, so as to make a spill-way, down which the water races vehemently, on a zigzag track. That is the salmon ladder, which in any state of the water these strong fish can pass—the zigzags giving them a point to rest on, and then shoot ahead again with every muscle working.

All the stretch down to the tideway is netted, but in the broken waters under the weir anglers get their chance. It is a curious appanage, and I doubt if any other European capital has the like within its city boundaries.

Not even I would suggest that the main interest of the Liffey lies in its salmon fishing. But I want to emphasise that past the quays of Dublin there flows a river which, however muddied and dishonoured it be in the last stage of its journey (and no river is at its best in a tideway), yet is a river adorned with all the attractions that belong to

Irish rivers and the wild life proper to them. Indeed it is not less beautiful, but finer and more varied in its beauty than most of its rivals ; and it has a kind of symbolic quality, because it sums up the advantages which Dublin possesses in variety of surroundings.

Two kinds of beauty are typical of Ireland, the beauty of its own special fertility and the beauty of its lovely wildernesses. There is the Ireland that is the hunter's paradise, of the wide grassy stretches and the big banks, miracles of galloping ground, yet never dull or monotonous, always with some far-off mountain background, always fluttered over by the skirts of some sweeping cloud. Lord Dunsany has written of it beyond all praising in his *My Ireland*, and better still in his *Curse of the Wise Woman*, and has suggested too how that fertility lies up against great stretches of primitive and irreclaimable bogland.

The Liffey comes through that Ireland, not indeed from Lord Dunsany's Meath, but from where

> The merry music of the chase
>   Floats up the festive borders of Kildare,
> And slim-bright steeds extending in the race
>   Are hither seen, and camping legions there.

The " camping legions " wear another uniform since Sir Samuel Ferguson wrote that ; but troops are still at the Curragh, and race-horses still in training there, Kildare's coverts still " hide the wary-gallant fox "; and past them the Liffey flows through limestone land where fine-bred horses show " the mettle of their pasture."

But there is the other Ireland, to many of us even more endeared : Ireland of the grey granite, glistening on the mountain side, Ireland of the immeasurable heather slopes, where " only God exults in silence over fields no man may reap "; and in that Ireland the Liffey has its birth—its twin beginnings. For on the western slope of the Wicklow mountains one stream rises from near Wicklow Gap, above Glendalough, another from Sally Gap near Kippure, and both are strong rivers before they join in a wide valley and flow together for a mile before they plunge down the waterfall called Poulaphuca—the Pool of the Demon Horse.

All up here is wild as Connemara, fit only for small mountainy sheep ; what the Liffey comes from is like what the Dodder comes from, or the little river that comes down to Bray through the rocky Dargle. But these others flow straight to the sea ; the Liffey, rising not much farther off, heads away west into the plains as if it meant to join the Shannon, and has gone far through the limestone land before it swings round in a great loop and finally issues in the valley by Chapelizod under the Phoenix Park, to where Dublin stands at the very point of juncture between the two Irelands. Five miles from the General Post Office will take you to grass land, say on the way to Malahide, which lets for five guineas an acre ; five miles to the hills beyond Rathfarnham where the land is chiefly of value for what grouse it breeds.

All the rich land on each side of the Liffey was part of the English Pale from the twelfth century on, but in 1803, when Robert Emmet rose, Michael Dwyer, with a remnant of the rebels from 1798, was still on his keeping in the hills : Kilmashogue, Three Rock and Tibradden, that you see at the end of a score of Dublin's streets, were still country of the Gael till the Military Road was driven through their fastnesses past Glencree and Callary to the mouth of Glenmalure and beyond.

Now, as I have pointed out, for nearly two centuries Dublin has been moving away southwards towards moor and mountain ; its spread northwards to the plains was soon checked. No doubt the river had to do with it. Once Dubliners decided to move from the swampy levels in the Liffey delta, they had to consider water supply ; the springs and streams in plenty came down from the eastward face of the hills.

Then about seventy-five years ago, a period of development set in. Tramways were started in 1864 ; and more important still, the Vartry River in Wicklow was captured and led into a great reservoir at Roundwood from which pipes carried it to another reservoir at Stillorgan, among the foothills of the mountains, five miles south of Dublin.

There was a source of supply nearer hand. The piped water had to be led across the Dargle river which comes out at Bray—a bigger stream than the Vartry. But Bray was already an important watering place, only ten Irish miles south of the city, and dependent on this river for its supply : while the Dargle itself was the most approved place for picnicking. In short, Dubliners spared the amenities of this lovely valley, and they did well. The supply which they captured was a supply of soft water off the peaty soil and the granite. For fifty years and more I have been coming and going between London and Dublin and never fail to experience the pleasant change to that softness in one's bath.

But it really is astonishing that through all these seventy years and more the Liffey should have been used by Dublin only as an estuary forming its port, and as a water-course disposing of its offal. Dublin, growing fast, has been left short of water. But the Liffey, which was once the dirtiest sight in Dublin, is now going to be a bringer of sweetness and light.

If you should make your way from Glendalough over Wicklow Gap—a lonely zigzag road, much channelled by rain—you will find the King's River flowing, a strong stream on its way, as you

THE MONUMENT TO SWIFT ERECTED IN ST. PATRICK'S
BY HIS PUBLISHER

VIEW OF SUGAR LOAF FROM SHANKILL
By Mrs. Lennox Robinson.

drive towards Blessington. If you drive out by
the Military Road to the cross roads at Sally Gap,
among leagues of heather, below Kippure, the
Liffey proper will lead you down, also towards
Blessington. If you go out through Tallaght and
Brittas to Blessington—climbing all the way, with
mountain slopes on your left, and to your right the
vast fertile plains spreading west and north in
every shade of green, darkened here and there by
cloud shadows, and merging more and more into
purple as the distances lengthen—then, about three
miles beyond Blessington, you will come to the
bridge below which these two waters, the King's
River and the Liffey, plunge together over the
series of cascades down into Poulaphuca. For a
mile down from the bridge the joint stream has
run in a deep rock-sided gorge so narrow that a
dam eighty yards in length will block it.

That dam is going to be put there. It will form
a lake irregularly shaped, high up in the hills,
about three miles long. Pipes taken from this
will be led to turbines at the Golden Falls, three
miles further down, where electricity will be
generated to supplement the Shannon supply.
Other pipes will lead water direct to the spreading
city and even north of it, to seaside places like
Malahide.

One blessed fact about such schemes is that they
make beauty rather than destroy it. That new lake
in a rather dull dip among the mountains will be

an ornament : and it will hold trout for the angler
in very large numbers. What is more, the salmon
fisher—justly made anxious by what has happened
on the Shannon—need have no fear. As things
are, salmon do not go above the Golden Falls :
they could not get up Poulaphuca. That is to
say, all their spawning grounds will be undis-
turbed ; and though there will never henceforward
be the wild floods which have swept down after
heavy rains, there will not either be periods when
drought reduces a mountain-bred river almost
to the bare bones of its bed. Water will be stored
and distributed, and nothing will be taken from the
amenity of the richly-wooded valley which your
road traverses if you drive from Dublin either
towards the Curragh or towards Maynooth. At first
the Phoenix Park makes the valley's boundary to
the north ; while opposite it, on the slope below
Kilmainham, is the " Garden of Remembrance,"
a new park laid out on a design furnished by Sir
Edwin Lutyens, for a memorial to the fifty thousand
Irishmen who fell in the European War.

Beyond this is Lucan village, with its Spa, to
which Irish patients are now returning after long
neglect ; a hotel provides very capably for com-
fort. The river here is set between demesne and
demesne : on the north bank Sarsfield Lodge keeps
alive a famous name ; the great leader of the Irish
Brigade who fell at Landen was Earl of Lucan.

Beyond here, a weir built across where there was

a natural rock barrier keeps a trace of very old
history : this is Leixlip, the Salmon Leap ; and
lax is still the word for salmon in all the Scandinavian tongues. The Lax-weir, above Limerick
and the Shannon, is another reminder of the
Norsemen's occupation.

All this landscape, river and bay, is organically
connected with Dublin. The city's amenities
include also command of the shore northward and
southward. On the north at Howth is still open
heath-clad mountain, beautiful in itself and com-
manding views of the rarest beauty ; and beyond
Howth is the little watering place of Malahide.
This shore, running north, has a long succession
of sand dunes, perfect natural golf links. Nearest
of these to Dublin, and actually within the bay,
is Dollymount, entered from Clontarf—so long
that there is a links beyond a links. The place is
also a bird sanctuary, and since no shooting is
allowed, you may see also plenty of hares disporting
themselves on the salt weed of the lagoon inside,
along with the sheldrake, duck, curlew, redshank
and wading birds of all kind. Beyond Sutton, where
the neck of land leads to Howth, is Portmarnock,
where championships are played. At Malahide
links are on both sides of the estuary, where swans
congregate so numerous that fowlers complain of
their tyranny over the duck.

Southwards, there is the shore to Dún Laoghaire
and so to Killiney, with its view on the Vale of

Shanganagh. Vigo Park here gives a marvellous outlook. Sorrento Park, near it, is embellished by a memorial erected to Dowland, the famous lutanist of whom Shakespeare wrote in the Sonnets. His real name was *Dubhslainge* or Dowling, and he came from Dalkey. Beyond Killiney is Bray, Dublin's milder Brighton. Inland from it the little river flows through the Dargle and Powerscourt demesne, and a complication of glen and mountain ; " the beat of them " is not in Ireland nor out of it. But this is a book about the city.

One note I may add. Among the first railways made in these isles was that from Westland Row to Kingstown. It was run for cheapness, largely over unoccupied slob ; and its terminus was formed on an embankment of very moderate dimensions. As traffic increased to these almost suburban country places, another line was run further inland, through Dundrum, from Harcourt Street, and in the same way it was provided with a banked up terminus. Since the traffic here is mainly passengers, not goods, no steps were provided to gain access by carriage to the platform. Westland Row, always growing in importance, had to have this ; but the access was and is dangerously bad. This is one of the problems in town planning which new Dublin has to tackle ; and which it will, we may hope, solve in such a way as to abolish the horrible metal bridge that blocks all view of the Custom House.

Of the other termini, Kingsbridge is handsome and well planned ; Broadstone, equally handsome and spacious, has been struck out of use, and traffic that used to come there now is switched to Amiens Street, the terminus for the north—a passable station. But some of it is pushed through to Westland Row, where it is difficult and dangerous for a motor car to approach, and difficult and dangerous to get away.

It is the part of wisdom for visitors from across Channel to leave or join the boat at Dún Laoghaire, making the journey by car or bus direct between the pier and their hotel.

CHAPTER XIII

THE SLUMS, THE HOSPITALS AND THE SWEEP

THERE is no use ignoring it : Dublin has always been a city of the miserably poor, and the misery was worst when Dublin had wealth and used it ostentatiously. Before the War a wise Benedictine said to me that he had never anywhere seen such display of extreme poverty except in Naples. " And in Naples they have the sun."

Money was better distributed before the War than in the eighteenth century ; it is distributed better now than it was before the War ; yet even in the year 1937 there were still fifteen thousand families in Dublin which had only one room apiece to live in—and not always the whole of one room.

It is possible that in ten years time this figure will seem incredible to any Dubliner who may pick up this book. Even to-day it is surprising, because all round the city streets of little houses are springing up on slopes of clean land. Out towards Clontarf—out towards Crumlin—whole colonies of slum dwellers have been transplanted, and omnibus services organised to take the children to school, and the workers to their work. They have been lifted mostly out of big tumble-down houses nearer the centre, built on swampy ground

where drainage was difficult ; and the neighbour-
hoods to which they have been moved are not
enthusiastic for their coming. Small boys who
never saw a garden before agree in their reaction,
which is to loot. Dublin of this generation and of
the next will have to pay off, bit by bit, the appalling
social debt piled up against the well-to-do.

People are busy all the time in efforts to level
up what is so dreadfully uneven ; and Dublin at
large is aware that a Protestant clergyman, Canon
Hall, has worked perhaps with more efficiency
than any other single person at the housing question. But the great Catholic Association of St.
Vincent de Paul has its workers everywhere, and
there are individual philanthropies. Not long ago
a party of us had gone to picnic on a beach, away
beyond the Malahide estuary ; and suddenly the
landscape filled itself with small active ragamuffins.
A singularly handsome young man moved about
among them, and was recognised as a famous
Rugby international ; we found that he spent a
good deal of his leisure taking out the newsboys
for country holidays. Probably that young foot-
baller was handling some first-rate human material.
I have known one man who began as a Dublin
newsboy : he was a sergeant-major when his
regiment reached France, he commanded a brigade
before the Armistice. And well I remember a
Dublin youth whose only avowed business was
prize-fighting. He looked a tough, though a

genial one, at all times ; but when we were all new to the job, I came round a traverse in muddy trenches, made worse by snowfall, just beside a disagreeable place called the Hohenzollern Redoubt ; and this fellow's large red face was like a sun through the mist. He had the kind of courage that spread itself over all about it.

These things need to be said because the most powerful pictures of Dublin slum life, Seán O'Casey's plays, definitely represent a city of worthless men held together by valiant women. Juno and her " paycock " are only the extreme examples : in the *Shadow of a Gunman* a little typist girl carries off the bag of bombs to save a poet and a tinker ; in *Nancy's Night Out* the drunken streetwalker downfaces a raiding party when all the men are putting up their hands. It is true that O'Casey shows also young men in trench coats, full of sinister enthusiasm, driving the less enthusiastic into danger at the pistol point ; but he does not paint them with sympathy. For a more balanced picture of the Dublin poor one should turn to a story written before revolution made the atmosphere hysterical—James Stephens' *Mary Make-believe*, which is also called *The Charwoman's Daughter*. There you have the charming little girl who has, like Juno, the quality of facing hardships with a gay heart, and of helping herself out with making fancy pictures ; but you have also the companion figure of a little man whose heart

SLUMS, HOSPITALS AND THE SWEEP

is big enough for a giant. There is a touch of
Charlie Chaplin about him—because he, like
Charlie Chaplin, is the kind of knight-errant whom
the world can laugh at and yet take to its heart.

Undoubtedly the most characteristic figure of
real life in Dublin to-day is the Lord Mayor, Mr.
Alfie Byrne, who has become almost a permanency
in the Mansion House and is kept there by the
votes of the poor. Nobody has ever seen him
without his gold chain of office ; it is as much part
of his make-up as his waxed moustache ; nobody
has ever known him refuse to be photographed,
and except a presidential candidate in the United
States or a film star, no one's features and figure
have been so widely broadcast.

But no one, it seems, has ever found his door
shut to the poor. It is not easy for any man after
twenty years of public life to retain a popularity
that rests on personal liking, yet the whole efforts
of Mr. de Valera's great following has been used
to dislodge the Lord Mayor and failed. Dublin
recognises and is loyal to an efficient never-failing
kindness : and I think Dublin has the feeling that,
if need were, their " Alfie " would make as good a
fight as his counterpart Burgomaster Max did in.
Brussels.

Very democratic members of Mr. de Valera's
party found fault with the Lord Mayor for appearing in evening clothes at a session of the Dáil :
they attacked him with being on his way to a

dance. But Dublin of the slums likes its Lord
Mayor to go to dances and shed the radiance of
his gold chain on as many partners as possible :
provided that next morning he will be ready to
listen to any tale of distress from the slums, and
help to set the law in motion on their side—or
possibly to prevent it from being set in motion.

Good works and gaiety must go hand in hand, to
please Dublin. One Dublin woman, very devout,
sets apart much of her wages for backing horses
in the interest of her favourite charities ; and
naturally, in the same interest, has become a great
student of " form." Errand boys, vanmen, coal
porters, tend to tarry at her kitchen door, consulting
her as an oracle, but also bringing their own
tribute of tips. One day she had been sent to a
doctor for serious consultation and came back after
some delay with a radiant countenance. " Yes,
miss, he says I'm to be operated upon : but isn't
it great ? that horse I was telling you about won
at fifty to one ? Isn't it the pity I didn't risk the
bob ? " Anyhow that was twenty-five shillings
for St. Antony of Padua.

I suppose there is nothing more characteristic
of Ireland than the Dublin Sweep. In a sense it
has fulfilled predictions : when the Free State
started, London was full of prophets assuring the
world that within a year a casino at Dún Laoghaire
would be competing with Monte Carlo. Indeed
in the eighteenth century, the Dublin parliament,

which was run by the Protestant aristocracy,
financed itself largely by lotteries. "Lottery
tickets will soon be Dublin's staple commodity,"
I find a paper saying, about 1784. But the Free
State Government of 1923, when it got to work,
developed a strong Puritan bias. One of its first
acts was to close all public-houses on St. Patrick's
day—and to pile up duties on alcohol. A proposal
to open gaming tables would have got short shift.

On the other hand, raffles for charitable purposes had been widely used, as far as was possible
within the law ; and one fact about the slum life
in Dublin was a distressing need for better hospital
accommodation. The agitation for a sweepstake
to finance the hospitals came from all quarters ;
one of Trinity's three representatives, a leading
doctor, was prominent in it. Mr. Cosgrave's
government refused to make it a government
measure, but agreed to leave the decision in
principle to a free vote of the whole House—party
whips being taken off. Mr. Cosgrave and Mr.
de Valera voted in the same lobby—and were
beaten. Since then the "Hospitals' Trust" has
brought in (by the end of 1937) eleven million
six hundred thousand pounds to the hospitals.
It employs in permanence two thousand three
hundred workers : at rush hours, before the Derby
or the Grand National, another thousand or so
are taken on.

It has stirred up human nature, no doubt not

always for good. But here is a pleasant story. The winner of a £15,000 prize came over from England to claim his money. The name for publication which he had sent in was " Inri " and he was asked why he chose it. He had always seen on his way to work the letters I.N.R.I. written up on a placard outside a church door. Not being a churchgoer, he had no idea what they meant, but it seemed a handy name. Since the prize came in, he had taken steps to have the placard nicely done up and painted. He was going back to his ordinary work as an engine-driver and a good deal of the fifteen thousand was already given away. But there was another thousand due to him because he had sold the book of tickets containing the winning number. He desired to make over this small extra luckpenny to the hospital fund.

That is the kind of man whose luck should thrive with him. When he came in with the news his sister, a dressmaker, had the room littered with pins and brown paper and he told her to throw the whole away. She said she must not disappoint her customers. " Very well," he said, " but when I come back from Dublin, never let me see another pin in the house."

Eleven millions and a half is a large sum ; but the applicants for a share in it were many and deserving ; if provision against illness were measured by the number of hospitals, Dublin would be well off indeed. But voluntary effort coming from many quarters has, in the nature of things, been somewhat uneconomically bestowed : and the effort has been all voluntary. Till the beginning of the eighteenth century practically nothing was attempted ; and when a beginning was made, the impulse came from those who most intimately knew the need—good doctors. It was extraordinarily forwarded by good women. The two oldest hospitals in Dublin are Mercer's and Steevens'. Mary Mercer, daughter of a Medical Fellow of Trinity College, was a contemporary with Grizel Steevens, twin sister of Richard Steevens, also a Fellow ; and under bequests from each of them the institutions were founded which still bear their names. Steevens' Hospital, near Kingsbridge Station, was built under direction of trustees appointed under Steevens' will : Swift was among them, and Stella, when she died, left part of her money to endow the hospital with a chaplain. The architect of the building was Thomas Burgh, who built also the great Library in Trinity College, and the fine barracks opposite Guinness's Brewery, which were for long known as the Royal, but now bear the name of Michael Collins. In building the hospital Burgh worked without fee or reward. Archbishop King, whom Swift never loved but always respected (" he is a wit and a scholar, but I hate him as I hate garlic "), supervised the whole from his palace of St.

Sepulchre's (now a police barrack) beside Archbishop Marsh's beautiful old library and opposite
Swift's Deanery.   Swift's own foundation, St.
Patrick's Hospital, for the mentally disordered,
was built after his death on ground ceded by the
older hospital.   Dublin, under Protestant rule, kept
pace with the charities of London : Guy's and
Mercer's are contemporary.   Sir Patrick Dun's,
the hospital specially allied to Trinity College,
was perhaps the oldest of all by intention ; for
Sir Patrick, a stout Scotsman, was with Schomberg
at the Boyne ; but litigation over his will deferred
till 1800 the actual opening of what Dublin knows
as " Paddy Dun's."

Catholic Dublin in the eighteenth century was
legally barred from any such public effort.   It
had not, it was not even allowed to have, churches.
An outlying quarter still keeps the name of Dolphin's Barn, because an old Quaker gentleman
used to lend his barn for the holding of services.
At the beginning of the nineteenth century the
misery of the Catholic poor does not bear describing. Two women were found to raise up organised
succour.   One was Mary Aikenhead, who founded
the Irish Sisters of Charity, the first Order of
unenclosed nuns permitted in these islands.   The
other, Catherine Macauley, her contemporary,
founded the Sisters of Mercy.   From Mary Aikenhead's work, under her direction, came St. Vincent's Hospital, Stephen's Green ; from Catherine

Macauley's, the Mater Misericordiae, on the north side, beyond what is now Parnell Square. When Florence Nightingale sought for training as a nurse she had to come to Dublin and get it under Mary Aikenhead's direction ; but the first nurses who went out to serve in the Crimea in Florence Nightingale's campaign were Sisters of Mercy from the Mater. Both these women worked under the direction and with the perpetual assistance of Archbishop Murray, whom the poor of Dublin still, I am told, after nearly a hundred years, remember as a saint. His statue is where it should be, kneeling in view of the high altar at Marlborough Street Pro-Cathedral on the edge of Dublin's slums. That part of his work which can be understood and valued by men and women of all creeds survives in the two great Catholic hospitals.

I wish I knew more of Catherine Macauley ; but Mary Aikenhead is of those who survive inextinguishably by a few characteristic sayings. Ostentation of piety did not please her ; she called the Sisters who were so affected, " holy pokers." When a newly-appointed Superior in one of her houses was frightened about her responsibilities, she wrote : " Do imitate St. Teresa and spit at the devil." Another came with a tale of woe about the difficulty of keeping peace among her subordinates. Mary Aikenhead contemplated her for some time, and then observed : " Thank God, my child, in all the bad things we ever did, we didn't marry." But the most charming saying of all is in her consolation to a novice who, serving in the refectory, let a great dish of mutton and turnips crash on the floor, and fled from the scene in tears. " My poor child, are you hurt ? " " No, Mother, but I broke the dish and left the mutton on the floor." " Well then, what about it ? If the mutton wouldn't go to them, couldn't they go to the mutton ? "

Out in Calabar Mary Slessor, the missionary, and Mary Kingsley, the explorer, did not find the night long enough for their talks. *Si qua fides dubiis*, there should be in another world place for valiant women with a sense of humour ; and Mary Aikenhead should have foregathered there with the Presbyterian and the Darwinian anthropologist ; and the three Maries, Irishwoman, Scotswoman and Englishwoman, should have great colloguing —not least about the wonderful workings of the Hospital Sweep.

As to the men, surgeons and physicians, Dublin, which has the Church of Rome, the Church of Ireland, and the Presbyterian Church, has its medical school of Trinity, its medical school of the National and its school of the College of Surgeons, each attached by various links to several hospitals. In each school and each hospital, every school and every generation of medical students has its hero and its heroes—not a few of

A TRUE DUBLINER

THE OLD CURIOSITY SHOP

them famous far beyond Dublin—men like Sir
Charles Ball, one of the glories of Trinity. But
writing now about Dublin, I am concerned chiefly
with those who were " characthers " of the city.
One such was certainly Sir John William Moore,
who seemed to me venerable when he told me I
was very young to think of getting married : but
nearly fifty years after I had achieved matrimony,
there he was, walking about the streets and looking
like old Time on an almanac. Yet during all
these decades, over and above professional cares,
he had been keeping an eye on that capricious
thing, the Irish weather, and reporting publicly of
its demeanour. Or again, there was Sir Thomas
Myles, a noted boxing champion in the eighties.
He and his brother Jack attended a political
meeting with other Protestant Home Rulers ;
there was some disturbance and opposition till
Tom Myles, a superb figure of an athlete, and
Jack, built like a gorilla, rose up and each took one
man under each arm and deposited them tenderly
outside and went back for more. But unanimity
had become perfect. To the end of his long life—
and I wonder how death got the better of him—
Tom Myles kept the same atmosphere of fine
strength and the candour of a great gentleman.

But in a Catholic city the most universally
known were the Catholics : there was Michael
Cox, known to all Nationalists by his life-long
intimacy with John Dillon ; they had been

students together in Newman's foundation. He had a handsome presence, with a love of letters informing all his speech. Richard Tobin, another pillar of Vincent's Hospital, was of the numberless Irish graduates who entered the Army Medical Corps and rose to distinction in it; but a long period of his life was passed in Dublin where he had, what is unusual, as many intimates among Protestants as among those of his own creed. Always a man of the world, yet he never hesitated to speak his manly mind on the most serious concerns of the inner life, without quibbling or controversy. It was entirely characteristic that when James Connolly, the Labour leader, lay wounded in 1916, with sentence of death waiting till he could be brought decently before the firing squad, Tobin, called in to attend his wound, entered into a real intimacy of friendship with the rebel whose action he had disapproved, but whose character filled him with respect and liking.

Yet none of these was so completely an incarnation of Dublin's special tradition in this profession as "Johnny Mac," the famous Surgeon MacArdle. Something rakish about his poise appealed to the Irish mind; but his own profession was lyrical about his unerring artistry. "His scalpel seemed to follow a line of light, invisible till he traced it," I can hear Michael Cox saying. And it appears that the poor worshipped him even more than his students.

Looking at it from a continental standpoint, the main significance of Dublin is as one of the most active centres in a world force—the Catholic religion ; and it may seem curious that a people so devout should have so few treasures of art to show which are connected with their worship. There is indeed an impressive number of churches, and even so they are all crowded on a Sunday ; still more are required. Yet not one of them all was built before the beginning of last century. Artistically, they are neither better nor worse than what was built by Protestants in the same period. And there is as yet no cathedral. The only thing to note of high artistic interest is the Palestrina choir at the Pro-Cathedral in Marlborough Street, endowed by a rich man of letters, George Moore's friend, Edward Martyn.

There is, indeed, the University Church in Stephen's Green, built for Newman's somewhat exotic germ that was to grow into an Irish University ; and exotic the building appears, after all the loving care and expense lavished on it. Newman himself, and his follower, Thomas Arnold, a desperate seeker after some sure anchorage, are fitly seen, white marble effigies, among all the columns and marbles of that richly ornamented basilica. But it lacks daylight and air. I cannot relate it to the general life of Dublin.

In the new Dublin there is provision and design already for a cathedral to stand in the spacious and well-ordered enclosure of Merrion Square; but the foundation stone is far from ready to be laid. The choice of a site in what may still be regarded as the wealthiest inhabited quarter has a meaning. When Merrion Square was built, not one house in ten was owned by a Catholic; now the proportion tends to be the other way. But the Pro-Cathedral was set where most need for it was felt, among the swarming population of the slums that extend from O'Connell Street towards the river and the strand.

All the recent books which deal fully and intimately with the life of Irish towns—Joyce's *Portrait of the Artist as a Young Man*, Conal O'Riordan's *Adam of Dublin*, Frank O'Connor's *The Saint and Mary Kate*, Seán O'Faoláin's *Bird Alone*—recognise, even when they are in revolt against it, how deep the Catholic religion exerts its hold. These writers, all of Catholic upbringing, do not hesitate to show the grossest and most debased debauchery among the Irish slum-dwellers; yet it is never a world from which religion has disappeared. Perhaps more significant than any studies in fiction is the story of a Dublin working-man who died in 1923, nearly seventy years old. For fifty years, while he did his work and earned his wages in a timber yard, he was practising austerities like those recorded of the early Irish saints. Christianity was accepted with passion in Ireland; but the native Irish saints gave to it a cast of ascetism that St. Patrick, the Roman Briton, never advocated.

Matt Talbot, born in 1856 in a working-man's family, was careless and drunken as the most careless till he was five-and-twenty. Then he told his mother that he was taking the pledge for three months—but, as he owned later, his intention was to break it. During the period of the pledge he lived a life of penances, imposed by himself; they fortified him in his reform and he went on steadily increasing the mortifications till the end of his days —to an extent that no one guessed at. When he dropped dead in the street on his way to church in 1923, and was taken to hospital, the Sisters of Mercy found chains round his waist and his limbs which had sunk into his skin—though the body was scrupulously clean. He fasted and prayed to an extraordinary extent, and neither boasted of the fact nor concealed it. At the yard where he worked, he never let bad language pass without a protest, and would go aside and pray in a shed to make reparation. It seems that he won, and that bad language disappeared. He was no leader in trade disputes, but when there was a strike he stood in loyally with his fellows. As his devoutness became known, he was constantly asked for his prayers, and some hold that his intercession had been effectual.

His earnings before the War were not so much as a pound a week, but more than half of what he earned he gave away. All this was known to all his fellow-workmen, though his chains seemed to have been concealed from everyone till his death disclosed them. But otherwise he lived the life of a Dublin working-man employed for thirty years in the same yard. Since his death steps have been taken to have him officially "beatified" and ultimately recognised as a saint.

During a great part of Matt Talbot's life Charles de Foucauld, who had been a brilliant but un-disciplined officer in the French army, and then an adventurous explorer, was practising away out in the Sahara austerities as fantastic as those of the Dublin working-man. Nothing positive came of de Foucauld's mission to the Touareg tribes ; but for him as for Matt Talbot the spiritual exercise was an end in itself—though he was still, whenever the chance offered, constantly a comrade of General Laperrine, who subdued the Sahara and its people, and who was anything but devout. Any instructed view of modern France must take account of de Foucauld ; it is a country which could still produce such a spiritual Don Quixote. And Dublin will not be understood unless Matt Talbot also is taken into account, as well as Mahaffy and Father Finlay, Joyce and O'Casey, Lane, Larkin and, above all, James Connolly, who, at the head of a Citizen Army of Dublin working-men went to join with Pearse in proclaiming the Republic, to defend the Post Office beside him, and to face, as Pearse faced it, the firing squad.

Nobody who knows about the life of Dublin or indeed the life of Ireland can be indifferent to this question of Dublin's slums : and it is worth while to examine a little one aspect of what is being done—for it links the new to the old.

Lord Charlemont, who sent Grattan into parliament as member for a borough which he owned, was rich and cultured and had all the means to live agreeably, but he was also public-spirited and felt bound to serve the country from which his wealth derived. He had made the grand tour elaborately, he had been part of London's most brilliant society, but his conclusion was that " Ireland can be served only in Ireland." To live on his estates in Armagh and Tyrone seemed impossible for a man with his tastes : he needed to be near a town and near the sea. So after providing himself with his mansion in Rutland Square, he bought land out towards Clontarf, running down to the strand, and called the place Marino. All that is left now of Charlemont's building is the charming little model of a Greek Temple, which served as a very luxurious summer-house. But if his ghost ever visits there, it must be surprised at the view. A long embankment carries the Great Northern railway across what Charlemont knew as tidal water : beyond that are to be seen long moles stretching seaward by the harbour, and built up on them are electrical works, grain elevators, oil tanks and giant cranes. All this apparatus of modern commerce is very fittingly placed on land recaptured from the sea. As to the estate of Marino, it has been for long in the possession of the Christian Brothers, who more than all other agencies put together offer chances of escape for those born in the slums. One fact about Dublin is that an immense deal of work in education is done there by men and women who devote their lives to the task without payment, in communities ; the Christian Brothers, a lay order, are specially the teachers of the poor. They teach religion of course ; throughout the whole of Eire every teacher is free to impart his own religious belief without limitation ; but the whole course of education is planned to the practical needs of life. I have known a Protestant clergyman complain that when a Protestant firm advertised for a clerk or shop assistant, the Christian Brothers had a team of applicants educated as if for that particular job. Ireland is being saved in Ireland in another way than by Charlemont's residence, and it must be said, a more practical one.

Across the rest of what was Charlemont's estate a network of new roads have been run, since the Free State was founded, lined with little houses : and the chief artery of this new suburb is called Griffith Avenue. Arthur Griffith, a Dubliner, and descended from generations of Dubliners, was a printer by trade before he became a journalist— bitter in attack, but always maintaining so fine a sense of literary form that many writers, from Yeats down, contributed to his paper, the *United Irishman*. He more than any other man led the revolt against the old Irish Party which carried on the fight at Westminster. Ireland, he held, must be served in Ireland. Revolution came, not perhaps as he had planned it, but the outcome of revolution sent him as the head of a delegation to meet Lloyd George and the strongest men of the British Cabinet in negotiation that lasted many weeks. When terms were at last threshed out which gave less than what Ireland was asking, but in Griffith's judgment enough to be accepted as fair, the English asked : Who will take the responsibility of recommending to the Irish Assembly to accept ? " I will, Mr. Prime Minister," said Griffith. This son of a Dublin artisan feared neither his own people nor the English. He was less concerned for a theoretically complete independence than to attain the point where he could go to work ; and assuredly one of the objects nearest to his heart was to remake Dublin, the city in which his life's work had been done. Rightly his name is commemorated in a quarter of the poor, but a quarter where the poor are decently housed.

Looking at Dublin from Marino, one sees all along the water's edge what is really reclaimed slob : good enough for factory sites, but very unfit for human dwellings. It extends on both sides of the river and readers of Mr. O'Flaherty's book, *The Informer*, will find lurid pictures of some of the life there. Much burning took place in Dublin within a space of seven years : unhappily many things that should have been preserved— like the records in the Four Courts—perished, and many things that would have been improved out of existence by burning escaped.

It is a slow process of improvement, but it goes on ; and attention is paid to placing new factories which have sprung up under a drastic system of protection. Several are along the road past Harold's Cross which leads towards the mountains, and new habitations for the workers are provided. In another case, which concerns the writer of this book more nearly, chance helped. A firm of printers and publishers established for almost a century had their printing works in one of the streets beyond Westland Row which runs parallel to the Dún Laoghaire tramline, well down in the slob. New machinery as it was required had been tucked into a square perhaps of an acre behind the little old office. Then in 1935 fire broke out and the whole was destroyed.

To-day, on the further bank of the Dodder beyond Clonskeagh, on a wide stretch of green pastureland, something like three acres is under new buildings full of new machinery ; motor buses take the work-men to and from their work ; and those who have had a hand in the printing, the illustrating and the binding of this book, work in as comfortable

DUBLIN LOOKING WEST FROM FIRE STATION

Bank of Ireland seen over Trinity College: St. Patrick's, Christ Church, and Dome of Four Courts in the distance.

conditions as could be desired. That is, I think, a pleasant and a typical fact of the new Dublin.

Dublin has always, since it was a real Capital, produced and consumed a deal of printed matter. Brewing and distilling also are old industries that have survived in magnificent proportions. But it was in the eighteenth century, even under tariff restrictions, a manufacturing city, and whatever it may become, it is not that now. The motor trade no doubt employs more hands than coach-building and saddlery used to need. But in the main Dublin is a distributing centre, and its shop-keepers attend to that. Visitors who want to know what is characteristic in our home products may find entertainment at the " Country Shop " in the basement of a great house in Stephen's Green, a few doors from the Shelbourne. Here is to be seen a selection of the best tweeds, home-spun or machine made ; here are Irish-made toys, some of them dolls modelled accurately on the Aran islanders' costume ; and what is more important, here can be had a perfectly good Irish tea, with a choice of the home-made breads which are characteristic and excellent. I cannot answer for their barn-brack ("speckled bread "), but shall set down plainly that this valued form of currant loaf is to be had in perfection at Messrs. Bewley's tea house in Westmoreland Street—where is also coffee that would be a credit to any house in any part of the Continent.

Gamble, the doctor whose sketch of Dublin in 1810 I have already quoted, remarks on the lack of good eating-houses as compared with England. Nowadays the principal hotels—Shelbourne, Hibernian, and Gresham—have restaurants giving meals of the more complicated sort, and there are good grills at the Moira, the Bailey, the Dolphin and other places. But one spot in Dublin combines so many other memories with gastronomic associations that I shall enlarge upon it.

Suffolk Street continues the line of Nassau Street westwards, and then reaches a bend where there is a short but marked slope to Dame Street, opposite St. Andrew's Church. This rise from the level of College Green is all that remains of what was once a large hummock rising out of the boggy flats. The Danes used it for their Thingmote, or outdoor parliament. There it remained till in the eighteenth century Nassau Street was being constructed to face the low-lying swampy College Park with a long embankment, and to get materials for this the top of this greatest among the Hogges was cut away and distributed. The nineteenth century built a church on this levelled site. Opposite the church, at the street corner, came into being a well-reputed pub— Corless's—which in the last years of last century had the best oyster bar in Dublin.

About 1905 M. Jammet, member of one of the

French families devoted to the art and profession
of cookery, found the Lord Lieutenant, whose
household he had accompanied, recalled by party
changes. During his residence in Dublin the
Frenchman had concluded that Dublin needed
a French restaurant. He bought Corless's; like
a wise man left the bar as it was, with its tradition
of oysters and lobsters served in all manners,
but set up a small room with good French cookery.
After the War the Hibernian Bank wanted an
office at this point, and bought out M. Jammet, who
moved to a more impressive site in Nassau Street,
with an alley leading from Grafton Street to the
rear of his establishment.

Dublin is well provided with fish, flesh, fowl,
and game, and at this restaurant, or in the grill-
room above it, one may find this excellent material
treated with the traditional art of France—and
a well-chosen wine-cellar at command.

But if I desired to partake in Dublin of a meal
whose excellence I could not match elsewhere,
I should enter by the alley at the back, abide at
the settle myself and ask Kelly to open oysters
for me as he used to do when the place was
Corless's and has been doing ever since. With
the oysters would be the usual condiments, accompanied by oatmeal biscuits made by Messrs.
Jacob, and draught stout. This stout is, it appears,
manufactured only for rapid consumption in
Dublin itself, and is to my mind the perfect

completion of pure oysters. They come from Galway Bay, where no pollution is possible, and they are for clean delicacy of taste quite unequalled. I said so once to the French *maître d'hôtel*, expecting him to correct my view, as he frequently did about wines. But he answered with a mellow gravity: "*Vous avez parfaitement raison.* They are the best in the world."

The extent of such a meal would be more likely limited by my purse than by my appetite. Things are not now as they were in Grattan's day, when, as I find from a note in the *Freeman's Journal* of January 9th, 1780, a gentleman agreed with a Carlingford oysterman to give him a shilling for as many oysters as he cared to eat. But after about a quarter of an hour, the first hundred had been swallowed, and then the second hundred, "in addition to a sixpenny loaf and a gallon of porter," and the customer was calling for more, when by the interposition of the company the oysterman was let off his bargain. Without desire to emulate, one may envy the opportunities which were so voraciously abused.

But, when all is said, Dublin is still a place where good living is to be had at moderate cost. When the Commission which founded the National University was sitting it lunched at Jammet's, and Henry Jackson, speaking with the genial authority of Cambridge, used to complain as he poured himself a generous libation of John Jameson, that we kept all the best Irish whiskey for ourselves in Ireland. The rest of us told him that he must allow for the atmosphere, which even Jameson could not export.

We all like to believe that Dublin has a charm of its own, which we encourage strangers to explore ; and we do our best to entertain them, according to our frugal resources, at the expense of each other's reputations.

INDEX